The Spiritual Mind

How to transform your awareness
and change your life

The Spiritual Mind

How to transform your awareness and change your life

Jim Ryan

Winchester, UK
Washington, USA

First published in 2011 by Brahma Kumaris Information Services Ltd,
Global Co-operation House, 65 Pound Lane, London NW10 2HH

The right of Jim Ryan to be identified as the Author of the Work has been asserted by him in
accordance with the Copyright, Designs and Patents Act 1988.

ISBN: 978-1-78099-377-5

A CIP catalogue record for this book is available from the British Library.

Design: Stuart Davies

Printed and bound by CPI Group (UK) Ltd, Croydon, CR0 4YY

CONTENTS

Prologue

"In the unlimited consciousness of the Supreme Personality of God, a thought manifests in the great mind archive of pure creative love.

Like a shimmering jewel, like an exploding rocket, showering its beauty and power into the ether of the subtle worlds, a starburst-thought of sacred energy enters the subtle soul-hearts of the sleeping earth-bound souls.

And this blueprint of God's pure intent is embedded deep in the subterranean depths of the soul's subconscious heart to lie dormant, hidden, waiting for the moment, the time of manifestation.

As the energy systems of the planet deteriorate, as the material support systems lose force and purpose and values and integrity crumble, pulled into the chaos of the collapsing fields, so in the hearts and minds of the fear-filled souls come pleas and cries for answers, help and an end to their pain.

And God hears this.

And from His compassionate heart center, a vibration of love is sent to touch, to activate the love thought seed, to stir these star sleepers of the spiritual way.

Caressed by the subtle waves of God's pure mind they wake, and so begin their search for the light source, the initiator of their call.

And journeying through the tear-stained lands, assailed and beguiled on all sides by the forces of illusion and aggression, each seeded heart is irrevocably drawn, guided and supported to their light launch center to finally unite and align with truth's eternal master plan."

Part I

What is the Mind?

In its purest form, the mind is a subtle energy and an integral part of the spiritual self. It is the vehicle that helps define and manifest our consciousness. Fed by emotions, external stimuli and the dance of interaction with others, the mind responds automatically by creating thoughts. From here the intellect becomes an arbiter, deciding whether or not to proceed with those thoughts, and in so doing, the ensuing action creates an effect on the subconscious mind. Continuous and repeated actions develop the patterns of our personality and nature. These then become major players in the type of thoughts that continue to surface in our minds.

The mind itself has been likened to a thousand different examples and symbols. Each analogy usually relates to a particular mind state and its effects. Imagine a quick-thinking, slightly chaotic mind and a picture arises of an unbridled, free-running horse. A turbulent and worried mind gives rise to an image of a stormy sea, conjuring a vision of a mind tossed here and there by anger and untold other influences.

In contrast, when we think of the idyllic scene of a peaceful lake set among nature's bounty, it symbolizes the peacefulness of a calm, serene mind. Or we might imagine a garden with its perfumed fragrance and ordered borders, exemplifying a mind that is virtuous, good-natured and content.

Each analogy gives us a particular insight into our feelings and inner makeup. Yet, with the plethora of symbols we create in order to grasp this phenomenon we know as our mind, many of us remain none the wiser to what it is, how it functions and its place within the overall scheme of living awareness.

Most will agree that the mind's main function is as a portal, linking the inner world of the self to the external world that surrounds us. Through perception and analysis that links the information and input we receive via the senses of sight, hearing, touch, sound and smell, it tries to make some logical and tangible sense of what it experiences and then deliver an appropriate and effective response, through either words or actions. The input may also trigger an inner reaction that may be connected to a past memory or a past experience or both, and the response to these triggers may be closely connected to the emotions and feelings that emerged at the time of the original experience. These actions may be spontaneous or carefully thought out. The latter occurs if the individual refers to the mind's guiding touchstone, the intellect, which, when consulted, considers and assesses and then makes a judgment on the evidence available. So, as the mind acts and reacts to situations and personalities, it triggers inner feelings leading to some form of physical response.

Once the mind decides to act upon its thoughts it moves into action. Yet this is not the end of the story as over time a new player enters our inner drama, that of habit or nature. The repetition of these acts creates habits and these in their turn become catalysts for further thoughts, leading to further types of activity and the development of a particularized nature.

As the mind repeats this spiral it moves into rotations of similar thoughts, similar perceptions and similar reactions. With each rotation it deepens the groove of those responses like the needle on an old record player that plays the theme tune of our nature. These reactive patterns quickly become habits, which then go on to dictate and form our attitude, nature and person-ality. They become our response to the world:

What we think is what we become.
What we become is who we are.
What we are is what we experience.

In its purest optimum state the mind works like a many-faceted crystal entity with each facet an effective working organ of awareness. The mind is a complex, yet subtle, machine with all its components working wonderfully and smoothly together to connect, interpret and respond at the highest level of awareness. This accuracy and clarity naturally brings the rewards of well-being, success and happiness.

But sometimes our attitude and vision become heavily influenced by a consciousness that has been created and formulated through an incredible battery of complex and diverse external energies. Our world, with all its technologies and wonders, is a product of man's great ingenuity and energy. Yet incredibly, and paradoxically, our attitudes and vision, how we see, what we think and what we actually do, is being dictated to us as a direct result of the very structures and forms that we have created. Just like Frankenstein's monster, we lose control, relinquish our authority and allow our creation to dictate our needs and feelings. The creation enslaves the creator. So, depending on our influences, we may be taken through the whole roller coaster of experiences: from great heights of euphoria and happiness at the next turn we can plummet to the depths of depression, sorrow and total confusion.

Where is Your Mind Right Now?

I believe, without exception, that we all desire to experience and bring the primal energies of peace and love into every aspect of our lives; we want to be able to understand and make sense of our lives within this ever-changing world. To me, this indicates that such harmony and awareness was once part of our inner nature.

When at times we find ourselves out of harmony – when things are falling apart and life's joys are in short supply – the majority of us will do as much as we can to seek our former stability and relative well-being. Think of the child, who having tasted strawberry ice cream will then constantly seek its wondrous joys. And even though he or she may have momentarily forgotten the taste of the ice cream, on glimpsing or smelling it again the memory is triggered and again the child craves its former delights. In the same way, as we become embroiled in the complexities and interplay of life, where worry and discord become the norm, we are shunted away from our spiritual world. However, a sound, a symbol or a slight, subtle experience can easily stir and reawaken these forgotten memories and feelings. And then we, like the child, remember and long for a similar experience, a similar taste. Sometimes we may even pull away from it through fear of the unknown and through fear of change or new demands.

The question often arises: why have we landed in such desperate straits? The image that comes to me is of the Marie Céleste. A ship with all its equipment, food and resources fully intact, yet without a crew member in sight; drifting alone and empty on the open seas, possibly as a result of some influence, either internal or external, that caused the crew to abandon ship. In the same way the human mind, while possessing all the qualities needed to travel forward on its journey of experience, may allow external or internal influences to take control.

In so many cases the mind abandons its inner truth in exchange for the false messages and promises of the prevailing religions of science and technology. It falls under the sway and glamour of external roles, physical form and fame, and like the crew of Ulysses' ship it listens for too long to the siren's call of false philosophy and false beauty, and loses command of the ship of its life. The mind becomes lost in the dense fog banks and heaving seas of materialism, consumerism and physical identity.

In this state, the mind desperately calls out for rescue. It looks for a way back to its natural state and all the while the boat of life drifts aimlessly on, tossed here and there by the turbulent, destructive waves of the world. In this Sargasso Sea of confusion, many pathways of support may appear to offer solutions. Yet as quickly as these lighthouses of hope and salvation manifest, once embraced, they quickly dissipate back from whence they came into the mists of illusion. For they, too, are part of the same artificial reality.

Yet, the voyage must continue. The mind is on a quest to rediscover its unique spiritual identity. To re-find the holy grail of its deepest yearnings – the hallowed sanctuary wherein dwells the sacred chalice of the soul's pure consciousness. But before this great reunion occurs the mind must go through processes of acceptance, relinquishment and renewal. It must go through many testing experiences and many crises of identity before it can finally wear the laurel wreath of self-awareness.

It's a journey, often long and arduous, dark and confusing, full of deception and untruth, where the mind struggles against frustration, anger and despair. The ensuing sections follow this drama as the mind, in adopting such costumes of consciousness like the stone mind, the hollow mind, the sponge mind, the fragrant mind and mannequin mind – in an often desperate hope that these attitudes will fit, will work – will answer its needs.

The Stone Mind

Heavy and ponderous, the stone mind crushes and lumbers over the worlds of sensitivity and subtle creativity. Often to be found enclosed in a tank-like, armor-plated world of self-righteous opinion and emotional indifference, its viewpoints and perspectives are narrow and limited. The stone mind's only way forward is with confrontation, running roughshod over others' lives and ideas. All counter-positions to its opinion are rejected and attacked, treated to the gunfire of aggression. There is no compromise and no prisoners are taken.

Attacked on all sides by the haranguing, cruel-tongued harpies of need, desire and accumulation, the once strong, proud and freethinking mind is soon overcome and left scavenging for scraps of experience at the high table of materialistic compliance. Through this constant and incessant battery of influences, the mind quickly loses its independence, confidence and awareness. Vulnerable, it becomes frantic in its quest to restore and reunite with its former sense of well-being. In panic, it starts to grab at and engage with everything and anything it encounters in a desperate attempt to reach the Promised Land, where all things are believed to be attainable. But being too easily manipulated and exploited, the mind is soon led into the wilderness of false hopes and illusory promises where it becomes lost, bewildered and empty.

The stone mind is non-discriminating and receptive and has little strength to resist the media of materialistic persuasion. When others readily proffer what seem to be authentic models of social aspiration and so-called success, it accepts them. These models are often crass, self-centered and socially aggressive, valuing materialistic accumulation above all else. They endorse an extreme fixation with looks and the body beautiful together with the number one priority to look after the needs of the self, which is valued as the most important and unique person in this or any other universe. These qualities are offered as the prime attributes and necessary stepping stones to a meaningful and successful life.

Though externalized and disempowered, and with no means of contact or without even an inkling of its inner world, the stone mind naturally and instinctively tries to find a way out of its dilemma. So, it starts to look and devise various stratagems in order to move forward into some sort of better state. However, having no access to its subtle powers of experience and discernment, the stone mind when it tries to cope and make things work starts to run on empty. Feeling threatened and vulnerable and needing support, it starts to copy and clone the mindsets and characteristics of these particular models and examples, clinging to the types of behavior and lifestyle that it believes will result in success and fulfillment.

Having been so persuaded, boorish, self-centered and selfish behaviors that are steeped in anger and fear become the norm. Nature becomes antagonistic and aggressive. There is an intrinsic urge to possess, to become and to achieve. Others are viewed as competitors or a means to satisfy personal ambition. Feelings and emotions become hardened, conscience is rejected and the mind gradually becomes locked and fixated, anchored to an impenetrable ego that is completely self-absorbed and driven toward self-promotion and self-aggrandizement.

The stone mind is totally driven by an ever-increasing feeling of insecurity and paranoia and by a fear of not being in control, thinking that others are always trying to take what it has accumulated. Cut off from its heart center, the needs, aspirations and feelings of others go almost unnoticed and ignored. Everything is pragmatically self-centered. There are no grey areas. The personal anthem of this mind is: "What's in it for me?"

As a result, the stone mind cannot be reached or breached by ordinary emotions. Appeals and entreaties to understanding, to compromise and to the heart fall on stony ground. Driven by fear, greed and self-importance, the stone mind will often exhibit, and even use, aggression and physical force together with the heavy, bludgeoning force of anger and negative body language to dominate and bully, often leaving others fearful and intimidated. This stance may trigger a response of deep frustration, confrontation and anger within others. And in return, the negative reaction of others further endorses and feeds the mind's negative opinions and aggression.

Away from its all-consuming struggles for control and accumulation, there are moments when the stone mind has glimpses of other realities: a subtle memory or a flickering image of some fond past experience. Yet these moments of inner sunlight only seem to highlight a deep, inner personal emptiness. So these windows are quickly closed and the weapons of interpersonal warfare are engaged once again.

Though ensconced in a castle of egotistical indifference, there does come a time when the stone mind is faced with the need to adapt and change to new demands and circumstances. It's at this point that the castle becomes even more of a prison. Its heavy and inflexible nature makes it very difficult, if not impossible, for the mind to effectively react and change in time. And like King Canute, who could not halt the tide, the waves of the new paradigm sweep on by leaving the stone mind isolated, abandoned, and completely ignored.

The Hollow Mind

The hollow mind is akin to a shell that, while outwardly attractive and fascinating, is empty inside. It can be compared with a once ordered and beautiful house that has become neglected and virtually abandoned. The roof is leaking, the windows broken, the paint peeling and the front door damaged and unable to close. Inside the rooms are neglected. What little furniture remains is old and in need of repair. Yet there is a lingering trace of its once grand former days, leaving the visitor with a slight sadness and a feeling of regret for what once was.

The gardens, too, still hold the form and pattern of former days, but disheveled lawns and flowerless beds that are no longer filled with beauty and attraction do not draw the admiring eye. So, with its original forms and qualities disregarded and forgotten, the hollow mind is left to search for beauty in the gardens of others. The house of the hollow mind is a place of emptiness – of evacuation. The owner has left and gone elsewhere, having been enticed by images and promises of better and more wonderful things.

The naïve and unquestioning mind receives subtle programming through the omnipresent and constant machinery of consumerism. More often than not this is firmly encouraged by family, friends and education. In this way, the mind is continually cajoled and enticed by the illusory external landscapes which claim that the attraction of wealth and position can bring about an ultimate, incredibly happy life. This illusory and fairy tale-type world is endorsed and validated by the pseudo-gurus of the media world, who pump out their trite innuendos of immediately attainable, wonderful and incredible golden tomorrows. Innuendos embellished with scare-mongering phrases such as: "If you don't buy-into this, imagine what will happen. You'll miss out, you'll be sorry!"

Trapped and deceived by the shimmering mirages of the solve-it-all promises of consumerism, the mind rushes with frantic abandon to embrace the projected dream. And yet all too quickly it finds that the shine and attraction is only a shallow, pallid glow of the glitter of a fool's false world. On discovering that the promises were empty and worthless and with little substance and devoid of experience, the mind is left angry and exploited, feeling abandoned and lost among the wide and barren lands of this spiritual desert.

The hollow mind is like a disappointed child. Frustrated and despondent and with little or no support, it is vulnerable and can become an easy victim to the hovering vultures of desire and a quick materialistic fix. Like the water-starved desert traveller, the mind desperately grasps at whatever is offered only to find emptiness in the panorama of mirages thrown at its vulnerable heart. Very soon everything is ripped away leaving nothing but the sad, pathetic remains of a totally dependent personality that is addicted to and dependent upon whatever is offered and whatever is suggested.

The hollow mind is readily enticed by external influences and drawn away from its essential nature and state of spiritual truth. When this happens it becomes like Sita in the Hindu epic of the Ramayana, who was deceived by Ravana who came to her in the guise of a golden deer. She left the protection of her home and was kidnapped. When external forms influence the soul, it wanders away from its true consciousness and so abandons its spiritual awareness and nature. Thus it is trapped in the outer worlds of change, physical form and attraction.

Lost and unsure, the mind adopts and follows whatever it discovers. On seeing the roles and forms of others, it imitates them and tries to become the same. Unsurprisingly this results in confusion, disappointment and sorrow. Having relinquished its true identity, the mind immediately experiences the loss of true awareness and understanding. This spiritual amnesia causes it to sever itself from its life purpose and from its ability to know and decipher its inherent blueprint of truth and inner guidance. For having chased the golden deer of transitory experience into the jungles of illusion, the mind becomes more and more lost, confused and ensnared among the plethora of false concepts and empty promises. And so the once mighty jewel of radiant consciousness becomes like an empty cylinder that can only echo its frustrations, fears and ultimate sadness.

Having lost connection with its true identity and nature, the hollow mind tries to replicate its inner beauty from a patchwork of perceived fits. Attracted by another's form or role, or convinced by the quick-fix propaganda of our time, the mind starts to clone and accumulate parts of other identities with the hope of achieving similar success or social acceptance. Yet this amalgam form has no strength or substance and if placed under any pressure it tears and falls apart like a child's tissue-paper model. As it adopts these traits, attitudes and external stances, the mind quickly discovers a huge misalignment, with things not really fitting, gelling or in any sense cohesive. It becomes like an actor who confuses another's part and lines with his own and as result everything goes wrong and falls into confusion. The wrong things are said, wrong choices taken, wrong directions followed and so on into chaos. Consequently a great deal of sorrow may be experienced.

At the best of times the hollow mind is hesitant and unsure, and regardless of need it will readily adopt the first forceful or coherent suggestion that comes its way. Like a frog, it jumps from one situation to another, from one crisis to the next, hoping for the best. And if no new direction is at hand it reverts to past choices and decisions. But the solutions of the past do not relate to its present needs and the mind quickly finds itself trapped once again in the same familiar quicksand.

The hollow mind's tendency to accept and follow with unquestioning zeal makes it extremely easy for others to influence and manipulate. With no guard of discrimination, it is completely open to the guiles and wiles of the predators of control and exploitation that inhabit the shadow worlds of deception and untruth. Whatever is promised, suggested or feasibly put forward, the defenseless mind gullibly and happily accepts, leading to entrapment and multiple misuses.

With no judgment or clarity to make sense of its present dramas and with no ability to synthesize and filter what is true and real, the hollow mind continuously replicates and repeats whatever comes its way. Just like an empty shell falsely echoes the sounds of the deep ocean, the hollow mind is full of false-hoods and wrong perceptions and readily spreads its illusions and compounds its confusions.

The Sponge Mind

Our in-your-face world demands an incredible amount of ready responses, resilience and boundless energy. As a result we spend much of our time simply coping and surviving. Like a struggling tennis player, playing the world's best, the balls keep coming from every angle and eventually we find it too difficult to return them, or respond effectively, and so we often just retire or even go under.

The sponge mind is formed in reaction to this. It is desperate to survive, to keep ahead and to meet the criteria of social and professional acceptability and success, regardless of its talent, qualities or skills. Under these huge pressures, the mind becomes like a sponge, constantly taking on board whatever it hears, sees and connects with, hoping beyond hope that the more it absorbs, the more likely it will be to find the answer – its meal-ticket upwards.

Each thought and idea, each influence that comes, is readily accepted and becomes part of its makeup, creating an incredible overload of advice and direction. Although this advice is usually given with good intention and taken with trust and high expectation, it creates a cocktail of confusion.

Spirituality teaches that each one of us is different and has a totally unique role to play. Each individual is centered in their own particular world, with their own unique requirements, and it is from this unique position that we interpret and interconnect with the flow of the drama surrounding us. Each person's perceptions and understandings are framed by their personal bias and how they see reality. Although the interpretations of one individual may be fine for himself – or herself – they may have no bearing on the needs and directions that others need to take. Their role and purpose in the world has a completely different orientation and direction. Thus, acting and following the lifestyle and footsteps of another only creates a mish-mash of misunderstanding and confusion that brings further disorientation and chaos.

So our sponge-absorbent, receptive mind, without any due discrimination, allows everyone and everything to become its guru – its guide. It is controlled by fear. Fear of rejection, fear of isolation, fear of failure and fear of not being accepted, which would mean a loss of status and respect.

A fatal open-door policy of accumulation is in operation, and the sponge mind is stuck in such a constant state of taking that it finds it almost impossible to say "enough is enough". Overladen and overwhelmed by too many thoughts, ideas and stratagems, it begins gradually to sink below the waves of clarity and awareness. And as it struggles to free itself from this slow, suffocating saturation, its plight is compounded by trying to escape through the only way it knows – by more accumulation.

This is a mindset wedded to the wisdom and superiority of others and blindly running and clamoring for advice, opinion and direction. And thus it becomes anchored and trapped in the murky depths of deep confusion, full of the denizens of unawareness with their half-truths and ferocious and ravenous fear of all things.

Lost in this tangled maze of numerous ideologies and strategies, the mind struggles to grasp and clarify the issues of life. Its purpose, direction, need and relevance become completely confused, leading to frustration and annoyance. Caught in this swirling eddy of repeating failed formula, the mind finds it more and more difficult to reach clear water. Despair, misery and hopelessness develop, as the mind seems incapable of forming any clear and effective ways to deal with the steadily increasing challenges of daily life.

And for the sake of social need and social face, the sponge mind, just like many of the inhabitants of the wine-dark seas, begins to adopt many colors and forms of attraction to compete with and attract those of its social world. In its desperation to know, the sponge mind creates an alternative subculture of learning and wisdom, gathering an incomprehensible world full of books, lectures and wise-worded acquaintances. In this subsurface world, the coral mind begins to lose contact with present reality. Seen only through the obscure lens of its altered state, its perceptions are cloudy and confused. Position, form and intention are continually misjudged and distorted. Things that are close seem far, those far away seem close at hand. The sponge mind seems to be always in a constant state of confusion, not to mention turbulence.

Outwardly the sponge mind may be a bon viveur, with a nature full of lightness, joviality and seemingly wise sagacity, but inwardly he or she is drowning in a sea of despondency and non-experience, constantly battered and depleted by the storms and waves of life's seemingly endless conundrums and predicaments.

The Fragrant Mind

The fragrant mind tries to see the best in all. It is appealing, good-natured and well intentioned. Meeting the fragrant mind, we easily fall under its spell. Attractive and beguiling, its charm draws us into feelings of immediate admiration and acceptance. Its words are sweet and positive, and seem so full of sense and good council that we readily acknowledge, follow and accept its guidance. In our present world, which contains so much aggression, confrontation and negative interaction, the fragrant mind arrives like a fresh, soothing wind and so we all too willingly embrace its words.

The fragrant mind loves the music of inspiring thoughts. It collects and repeats the neatly packaged formulas of the bland, the obvious and the deep. So often swayed by status or by force of argument, or more often just swept along by the waves of sentiment or misplaced emotion, the fragrant mind will willingly accept and wear the mantle of another's way and espouse others' opinions and judgments. When strong opinions do emerge, the fragrant mind is torn by its timidity, its fast-weakening resolve and its fabricated image of cooperative coexistence. So with great relief it quickly lets go of its mini-maelstrom of agitated opinion and resumes its comfortable stance of benign non-interference. For above all, the fragrant mind is good-hearted and wants the best for all. It is a consciousness formed and framed by a need for harmony and peaceful relationships.

However, the fragrant mind has been traumatized by past experiences of hurt, rejection, failure and manipulation. Behind the façade of good-natured well-being is a huge anxiety that the terrifying specters of the past will once again reappear. So the mind, with fearful trepidation, dares not and will not venture deep. It will not confront or commit itself to open the doors to new experience, nor plot a journey into self-discovery, fearing that it will once again be faced by the demons of its inner fears and the possible loss of its present acclaim. It is driven by the thought and desire of being accepted, of being loved and of all being well.

As with the other mind-states, with no access to its inner world, the fragrant mind has no inner support, no awareness and no spiritual strength to guide and anchor its life, and so it exists on the surface of experience. Having no roots or real depth, when pressurized and confronted by the myriad counter-beliefs of a global materialistic society, its hopeful, moral positivity is quickly overridden and abandoned to the prevailing barren landscapes of illusion. It merely follows the strongest views of the time.

Just like a delicate blossoming flower that opens to the warming sun, adding its beauty and its scent to the harmony of the garden, the fragrant mind also brings its own color and effect. But being fragile, sensitive and over-needy, the fragrant mind is extremely delicate and vulnerable to any form of influence and change. It is a butterfly that flits from one attraction to another, courting support, guidance and occasional meaning. Its commitment is only to the moment; just enough to satisfy its transitory and superficial nature. Beyond this dilettante spirituality, there is a desperate yearning for a deeper commitment and experience, but the risk and fears appear too great, so the mind stays within the safety net of its limited and constantly narrowing world.

When circumstances change and energies begin to fluctuate, causing the cold winds of adversity to blow heavily in on its life, the fragrant mind soon loses any resolve, focus and high intention that it may have had. And so it quickly retreats to what it believes is the safety of the shadow worlds of self-preservation, mediocrity and acceptable levels of popular hearsay. So, with limited awareness and little spiritual power, like a lemming it is swept over the cliffs of populist belief into the seas below, where there is no understanding, no experience and consequently no life.

The fragrant mind, being unable to cope with the continuous waves of negative effects, begins to lose its beauty, charm and resilience. Feeling tired, exhausted and abandoned it retreats sadly to the backwaters and to a life of repeated cynicism and distorted memory.

The Mannequin Mind

Feeling naked and vulnerable, the mannequin mind's need is to adorn itself, to give itself meaning and identity. It is driven by a desire to accumulate things. Then like a fashion show model to pose and show and strut that form. But one of the many disabling repercussions of buying into the materialistic philosophy of accumulation is that it can create an overload that completely swamps the mind, affecting its ability to assimilate information and act on it appropriately. For the mannequin mind, acquisition is the maxim or force to be followed. It picks up whatever it encounters and pulls it into the planetary orbit of itself. Regardless of whether there is a use for what it gathers, it must make a place for everything and so what it collects becomes part of the furniture needed for a life of accomplishment and success.

As it gathers and collects up everything that it senses, the mind is bombarded and rained-in on from every angle and rather than running for the hills to seek relief it acts a like a rabbit bedazzled by the headlights, placidly accepting its fate. The mind willingly and desperately embraces the quick fix of consumerism and gradually its self-esteem becomes undermined by the constant purchasing litanies proclaiming the need for betterment, improvement, success, status and beauty. Everything is accepted, to doubt is to sin. To reject anything would see it cast out from the

Aladdin's cave of instant gratification and be left to face an existence of emptiness, non-acceptance and failure.

Presented with this kind of external pressure, the mannequin mind finds it almost impossible to resist anything it encounters, whether that be relationships, moral choices, philosophical strategies or simply choosing a sofa. With so much choice the mannequin mind finds it equally impossible to discern a clear course of action, since making a decision would mean relinquishing other possible avenues of success and attainment. In such situations the mind becomes overwhelmed and extremely confused. It experiences a mental paralysis or situational checkmate. So, when doubts creep in, the uncertain consciousness reverts to its habit of absorption and its difficulties deepen.

Like a chocolate addict in a sweet shop, the mannequin mind grabs onto anything it can get its hands on, hoping, trusting and believing that it will lead to the promised Valhalla of a life full of happiness, perfect relationships and financial prosperity. As the profusion of possessions and fanatical obsession with physical beauty fail to deliver their paradise-like promises, feelings of frustration and hopelessness start to build. Yet the mind remains addicted and committed to the belief that external solutions will help and just as hope springs eternal, it continues this path. But being unable to cope and full of heaviness, worries and rampant fears, the mannequin mind gradually sinks beneath the waterline of well-being, overwhelmed by the weight of its overloaded world.

Yet the mannequin mind is nothing but resilient. Although trapped in its prison of choices, it will try to use them to rationalize and re-establish its position. With this profusion of options, but with little or no discrimination and almost no faith in its ability to affect a positive result, the mind will generally resort to a throw-everything-at-it, solve-it-all approach. Having a fear of losing it covers all bets, but coming to collect the winnings it has no idea which horse has won, which approach, which idea, or which way has worked, which brings further confusion, anxiety and a further sinking beneath the waves of awareness.

With the exits blocked, the mannequin mind becomes trapped in a subterranean existence and unable to meet its own needs. So the ever-resourceful and ingenuous mind begins to fabricate an alternative reality – a fantasy world where it plays out its desired outcomes. Here it achieves its desires, overcomes problems, is successful and becomes the hero of the story and the center of attraction. Within this fantasy there is no confusion or frustration or failure.

The more the mannequin mind allows itself to embrace this fanciful dream-world of imagination, the more it disappears from and loses hold on its responsibilities in the outer world. Eventually, everything else becomes of secondary importance as it gives itself up to the narcotic fumes of its illusions. Reality, and life, drift slowly away on a river of forgetfulness.

Part 2

Return to the Spiritual Mind

We have seen how a lack of awareness and the making of wrong choices allow the mind to develop many types of malfunctions. The forms and natures of these malfunctions are framed and fed by seemingly ever-present fears and worries and numerous accompanying thoughts and emotions.

Wrapped within and trapped by the heavy clothes of frenetic, negative thoughts, the mind longs to escape and reach the safety and inner sanctuary of peace. Yet it finds it extremely difficult to step away from the leach-like hold and incessant spinning of its fears and worries. In this state, the mind is powerless and despondent, with little thought or even desire to attempt some form of spiritual regeneration. Yet from time to time, perhaps triggered by a particular sound, word or simple interaction with another, feelings and memories manifest from this vague and nebulous inner world. A subtle, long-forgotten song begins to play, reviving and pulling the mind inwards, calling it to reconnect and align once again with its long-forgotten, but cherished dreams.

And as the consciousness begins to stir and old memories return, there is a desire to rekindle and reignite the inner light of awareness, peacefulness and natural harmony.

It is the signature of silence. A call from the subtle mind, from the eternal soul-self, manifesting the universal spiritual need of all conscious beings to experience a deeper understanding and an alignment and integration with its true nature and form.

When fed by its innate energy of awareness and power, the mind is able to function multidimensionally in a state beyond influence. It is free, light, and completely independent and self-sufficient. In this clear, pure crystalline form, the whole and complete consciousness of the mind operates and works unilaterally through its body costume. With a unified inner world of virtues and spiritual powers and having in its awareness an understanding of causation, the mind is equipped to respond correctly and effectively to the demands of the spiritual journey.

When there is a proliferation of unnecessary and wasteful thoughts, a state of confusion and discordance occurs. Yet, it is through silence that the mind can begin its journey back to healing and empowerment and return to the power and beauty of its former state – the spiritual mind. For in its original and perfect form, the spiritual mind is completely peaceful, aware and divine and is an image of intrinsic and natural beauty.

As in nature where the inception of new life is nurtured in the silent underground caverns of its inner world, so too must consciousness place itself deep in the soul's inner world, in the dimension of spiritual silence and peace. There it must remain to allow the subtle energies of pure consciousness to be revived. In this state, the mind is like a caterpillar that, prompted by its future form, responds to its subconscious and eats, assimilates and then cocoons itself, so that in the hanging silence the butterfly of its future beauty can develop. As the mind withdraws from external influences, it begins the journey toward self-awareness. As it feeds on the food of spiritual insight a revival occurs – a restoration of its original consciousness.

In this inner, reflective world supported by knowledge and the emerging powers of the soul, the mind experiences a reawakening of its ancient spiritual past. In the nurturing arena of deep silence, memories of an older time are stirred, evoking a time of ancient, elevated experience. This releases ripples of wonder and awe that shake and question the old, tired structures and supports of the mind's outer world. And as the ephemeral shadows of a distant past start to coalesce into a recognizable and tangible awareness, and as inner experience starts to permeate the mind's outer world with dramatic effect, the cloying hold of physical consciousness begins to weaken.

As the mind learns more and more to stabilize its awareness in this inner world, it starts to be influenced by the energy field of this original consciousness. For as the primal energies of love, peace and bliss work their healing ways, the mind's negatively influenced and confused nature starts to be mollified and dissipated. The long-term tendencies of pessimism and criticism start to be softened and dissolved, replaced by a natural upsurge of lightness and positivity. This freeing from the stranglehold of physical consciousness by the gradual filtering of subtle influence starts a revival of momentous repercussions.

Previously, the intellect, ignored and overridden by the demanding and domineering presence of the sensory habits, could do little to support or guide the mind, which bereft of its protection soon yielded to the tyranny of the senses. And just like a giddy infant, the open and vulnerable mind quickly fell into the stormy seas of sense gratification and spiritual emptiness. As a result, the intellect was banished like a forlorn ghost to the furthest recesses of unawareness and left there, forgotten and unused in its spiritual limbo.

With the coming of the new dawn of spiritual awareness the flickering glow of truth's eternal light soon spreads to bring new hope and new strength. And like Orpheus returning from the underworld, bathed by spiritual vibrations the intellect begins to be revived and restored to its former position of discernment and control.

As memory and nature are clarified, the restored intellect reminds the soul of the need to maintain and to strengthen this newfound freedom. So in its role as guide and teacher, the intellect begins to stipulate the need for information and understanding about itself and the nature of spiritual consciousness, emphasizing that a constant inflow of spiritual knowledge is crucial to the survival and development of the newly forming mind. It becomes its lifeblood, developing awareness and power, and acts as an anchor to hold it securely within the protection of the inner realm. And all the while a form of great beauty develops in the inner mind. Within the chrysalis of pure consciousness a great power is growing and being nurtured, awaiting its release and its manifestation in the world.

Discovering Meditation

Meditation is the avenue to God. It is the awakening of consciousness, the revival of power and the regeneration of love. Meditation is the pathway that enables us to let go of the old. It is the energy that revives and refreshes our tiredness, our hope and our will. It teaches us not only to begin to love ourselves, but opens our heart center to the world around. This inner journey is one of self discovery, a means to access our own spiritual treasures, which become stepping stones to the immense powers of God. This union of the soul and God is the key to personal change. It's a fantastic empowerment through which spiritual energy floods our inner self, healing and reconciling the past, focusing on that which is important in the present and preparing the us to move to a future that is assured and benevolent.

Meditation is an ancient practice, but its relevance has never been stronger than today. It provides a very effective tool to help us deal with many of the trials and tests of the everyday world and it's so simple to do.

Getting Started
- Find a quiet place and relax.
- Sit comfortably.
- Gently withdraw your attention from all sights and sounds.
- Become the observer of your thoughts.
- Gradually your thoughts will slow down and you will begin to feel more peaceful.

- Create one thought for yourself, about yourself – for example, "I am a peaceful being."
- Hold that thought on the screen of your mind; visualize yourself being peaceful, quiet and still.
- Now let us extend this experience using the following thoughts:

Meditation

Moving away from the demands
And needs of our chaotic world,
I slip into my inner world,
Into the quiet, still room of the mind.
It is a place, a space of calm, stillness and peace.
Here, I can let go of my concerns, worries and constant fears.
In this dimension of silence,
In this plain of peace, the incessant voices grow distant and
    quiet.
And in this arena of inner calm and soft serenity,
my racing thoughts begin to slow down,
begin to lose momentum
and soon are absorbed into that inner peace.
I am surrounded by silence,
by peace.
And that soft vibration soothes my mind and calms my
    thoughts.
I am held in that spell of tranquility,
I am bathed in the inner light of the inner self.
I float and drift in this sea of peace.
For here the waves of the world cannot come,
And I feel light and free and calm.

The New Consciousness

For a long time our perceptions and experiences of the world may have been based on the filtered programming fed to us through the masks of physical identity and the views and information engendered by philosophy and media bias. Catastrophically, if we believe these wholeheartedly and follow them fervently, we fall asleep spiritually as if under a wizard's spell and we then lose self-awareness, power and our connection with truth.

However, knowledge of our inner spiritual world comes to us like a rescuing prince giving us the kiss of life required to revive our flickering consciousness. It is through this reawakening that the inner light of an ancient and pure memory splutters into life, reviving thoughts and feelings of wonderful elevated times. It develops a sense of hope and a new vitality, as in springtime when the reviving sun stirs and reactivates the earth's long-dormant energies to bring new life in the form of new seeds.

With the new consciousness of spiritual liberation, the mind, having been so long imprisoned in the servitude of wrong direction, wrong advice and wrong actions, is released into the unlimited freedoms of inner silence. Here it is able to shed the heavy shackles of religious dogma and the mind manipulation of the ruling corporations and explore the vastness and joy of spiritual self-awareness by diving deep into the inner seas of peace and spiritual understanding. Through this spiritual self-expression the mind's innate nature is allowed to gradually show itself. And with recognition and acceptance it begins to integrate its newly cleansed and receptive superstructure. Seated within the casket of its new evolution, the mind is able to process and develop its awareness and its journey, guided by the recollection of a clear and revived intellect and empowered by the vast energy and love of the Supreme.

When the sleepy veil of old consciousness begins to fall away, the awakening mind begins to think and see with much more clarity and understanding, and soon the illusions of falsehood are quickly recognized. And from this gestating inner world, like a rising leviathan, a wonderful spiritual beauty emerges and a great, new power is released in to the world.

Thus the old spell is broken. And this new strength and new force pushes the consciousness Atlantis-like into the life stream of waking awareness. Let us sit in silence and meditate on this for a moment, repeating these thoughts:

Meditation

"From the external world,
from the external mind,
I venture inwards into the silent, inner lands
that so often rage with fast-flowing thoughts
and turbulent raw emotion.
Yet now, in these subtle lands,
and with awareness and attention
all extra thought and activity soon begins to recede and diminish,
and there emerges a calm.
A soft, subtle flow of soothing energy,
a balm, percolates into every pore and crevice of my soul's spiritual
  consciousness,
bringing a feeling of ease and peace and inner well-being.
And now I consciously hold this feeling,
this state of peace.
I hold and embrace this divine, sacred stream,
for in doing so I relinquish the energies and vibrations of external
  consciousness
and I experience a wonderful feeling of lightness and clarity
flowing, moving through my mind.
And there stirs deep within my spiritual form,
my pure, original energies of spiritual peace and profoundest love
and the awakening beauty of eternal truth."

Seeking Liberation

Although formerly blocked and choked by the debris from its past, once exposed to the soul's pure energy center the mind begins a cleansing and rejuvenation as powerful spiritual energies manifest within the soul's deep, subconscious nature. When it is no longer anchored to the shores of the past or to the golden promises of a would-be, could-be future, the mind is free to float in the sublime inner seas of awareness and deep spiritual peace. It is this profound calm and subtle clarity that enables the mind to recognize itself and to understand its nature and real needs, thus helping it to free itself from the illusions of unawareness that caused so much sorrow.

Centered in this inner world, the soul creates the necessary conditions for the awakening of truth and the development of pure consciousness. With spiritual understanding, focused thought and a pure desire, the mind allows its hidden light and its original power to come to the surface of waking awareness. And slowly, step-by-step, the jigsaw pieces of the spiritual mind begin to fall into place. As the mind holds itself in this subtle arena and starts to lift itself away from its old-conditioned consciousness, the spiritual framework of unity, virtues and understanding begins to be established. In the nurturing chrysalis of its inner world, the mind awakens and emerges with awareness and power then gradually moves into deeper aspects of spiritual understanding and experience.

As we have observed, the mind has been spiritually blind, unaware and oblivious to its condition. Yet as sight and old memories start to flicker and return, the mind begins to glimpse a wonderful beauty as an incredible spiritual world opens itself to the gaze of the newly awakened consciousness.

However, this awakening to the new consciousness of the spiritual places the mind in its most vulnerable and challenging state. In its newly nascent state, the mind often finds it difficult to hold the wonder of this new dawn. For still wracked and influenced by its old mindsets and illusions it may seem all too much, too unattainable and too difficult. It may appear as yet another trick from the propaganda of the illusory world of sorrow. It is then that waves of low self-esteem and hopelessness may return to draw the mind back into the clutches of its former demons.

There is help and support in the form of spiritual knowledge. Just like Ariadne's spider thread, this guides the mind out and away, freeing it from its Minotaur's maze of personal fears, worries, confusion and wrong choices. As spiritual knowledge filters into the gloom of unknowing, the mind starts to gain a clearer awareness of the path forwards. Yet it is not out of the woods yet. It is at this time that the mind is often faced with a great predicament: either to hold onto what it was and had, or to let go and move ahead and grasp a new, but uncertain world. At this life-changing crossroads the mind can find itself transfixed in a limbo-like state, frozen by indecision and fear. When there is the possibility of sinking into a fearful inertia and spiritual paralysis, the power of spiritual awareness acts as a life preserver by buoying up and supporting the floundering consciousness.

The power of spiritual awareness is all about connecting and reviving the long-forgotten and ancient truths that each soul carries in the deep memory-archives of its subconscious spiritual DNA. For spiritual knowledge, like the Norse gods' sweet nectar of eternal life, enters and flows into the long-dry channels of the soul's world to revive and restore life to the corpse-like consciousness of the physical mind. Spiritual knowledge is the *prana* or *chi* – the oxygen – of spiritual existence, energizing and illuminating the soul's heart center. And deep within this sacred center of the soul the fabrication – the structure – of an ancient time stirs and is remembered.

Having been fed by the sacred inner river of the soul's original spiritual powers, the now transforming and evolving mind arrives blinking and spluttering into the dawn of a new life just like a new infant. Everything around seems wonderful, yet at the same time strange and different.

It is at this time that the evolving spiritual mind will face its first and probably greatest test of faith. For in this pure, yet still fragile state, the mind is quickly assailed by the forces of its former world and attitudes. They come wave upon wave to attack the new and vulnerable mindset. Echoes and vibrations of the past flood its consciousness. Old voices, familiar sounds and faces appear like benevolent specters, pleading and cajoling: "Come back, it was fine, you've lost your way, it's been a mistake."

These mental images emerge like fond old friends pulling at the emotional strings of sentiment and selective memory. And from the ocean of the world also come waves of public opinion and societal norms, disapproving and warning of social isolation, rejection and eventual catastrophic financial loss. Bombarded and wracked by this incessant onslaught, the mind is liable to be so full of doubts and fears that its new direction and focus is in danger of being abandoned.

Though initiated by the seed of spiritual memory, and supported and nourished by the resurgence of the soul's life energy, powers and qualities, the mind is not alone as it is lifted into the womb of liberation. This process of becoming is overseen and orchestrated by the eternal birthmother of all souls. The Supreme Soul, like a caring, attendant midwife, becomes the subtle guiding energy – the supportive soul mother – encouraging and aiding the mind into its new world and consciousness. Just as the vast energy of the sun opens the sealed and waiting world of nature, so the unlimited power of the Supreme Being, love-driven and committed through karma, is the subtle surgeon that helps to facilitate the delivery of the expectant mind into the world of spiritual light.

Let us reflect on this process so far by sitting in silent meditation and repeating the following thoughts:

Meditation

"In my inner silent world,
calm and at ease with my emotional heart,
I reflect on my journey so far.
I have awakened to the effect of the agencies of external influence.
I know that though they may seem
benign and supportive,
ultimately, they sabotage my spiritual quest for oneness and well-being.
For my journey is inwards.
My quest is to discover and align
with my sacred center.
To experience the flow, the power and the beauty
of my soul-form self.
To allow the inner river
of love and peace and light to flow
into the sad, dry lands of my inner soul.
And I do this.
I allow this experience to take hold
And to irrigate and fertilize my awakening world.
I also realize that my journey,
my growth has been nurtured and supported,
When the shadows of the past have come, when old fears and weaknesses resumed their part,
I know that I have been helped.
For with me always has been the Supreme,
whose subtle love and pure vibrations
were constantly empowering and encouraging me,
giving me the strength to continue.
I know this,
and I give thanks."

The Growing Mind

Just as in its early years a young child is given protection and support, the mind too, following its initial spiritual awakening, needs the same type of care and guidance. At this time in its evolution, the mind is in much need of love and reassurance rather than major debate and confrontation. Thus, it is in the nurturing arena of silence and in the safety of its subtle world that the spiritual mind is able to grow and develop. In these inner seas of peace and love, the soft healing and revitalizing energies soothe, embrace and nurture the newly forming consciousness.

In this subtle state the mind is more open and receptive to the powerful love-vibration of God's pure energies. It has the capacity to recognize, to hold and to enter the light-beam of God's vibrational love, which, when connected with, immediately surrounds it with its protective power and vast pure consciousness. The turbulent and emotional energy fields that came in the mind's initial days of awakening are soon absorbed and changed in that huge ocean of spiritual power. The external chaos of doubts and old fears all begin to subside. Stability and awareness are able to return. The mind is then able to reconnect with its true spiritual center and draw that pure energy directly into its life-force, flooding every part of its consciousness with the soul's original power. Re-energized and reassured, the mind can continue along its new path toward its new reality.

As it moves into realignment with its perfect form and perfect consciousness, the mind starts to discover and savor the many wonderful experiences of realization and inner fulfillment. Just like a child at a party who is aware that everything is now available to it, the mind delights in sampling all that it comes upon and dances with a joy unrestrained. Deep within the soul's pure consciousness there is a realization that what it had long desired and searched for has been found.

Yet, there are many dangers and pitfalls for the newly formulated consciousness in these early stages of growth and development. In its initial stage of transformation the mind is vulnerable and can also be naïve, especially in understanding the process of its own change and development. In the enthusiasm to embrace spiritual change, it is important to remember that there needs to be a good degree of thought and reflection concerning the consequences of impulsive feelings and ideas.

Just like a toddler, the mind may have a tendency to become childish and irresponsible, often letting go of virtually all it had previously acquired, including common sense. This behavior can lead to later regret. Judgment and discrimination can often be impaired by euphoria and overconfidence during this initial rush of awareness and power, like the mouse who found a grain of wheat and thought itself a greengrocer.

As the mind begins to adjust to its new spiritual attitude and responses, the former restraints it had placed on itself are suddenly loosened. And because the new consciousness is not yet fully embedded and secure, it often unwittingly allows the old negative patterns to resurface, resulting in a tsunami of strange feelings, thoughts and emotions, which pour into the mind from the subterranean depths of its deep subconscious. This onslaught brings a repertoire of disabling effects, which to the inexperienced and unaware mind are often disheartening, confusing and possibly extremely upsetting. The mind may find itself troubled with thoughts such as:

"Is this the result of my spiritual endeavors?"
"Is this all there is?"
"Life was better before."
"I don't need this."

For the newly emerged consciousness, the company and advice of like-minded and experienced souls is of great help in these early days. They themselves have likely faced the same dilemmas. And together with experience and a wider view of the process and demands of the spiritual journey, their companionship, insight and support can give the hesitant and confused mind much needed confidence, blessings and power.

This resurfacing of the residues of the old consciousness is a natural part of the soul's process of inner cleansing. It is part of the final farewell to its illusory past as old behaviors return to bid a final adieu, enabling the consciousness to begin its flight into ascension.

Meeting the soul's former nature can propel the mind into a battlefield scenario where it fights off the ousted factions of the past who come to make their last stand and desperately try to regain their earlier positions of influence. It is at this point in the mind's evolution that engagement in battle could be extremely damaging. For without the necessary strength and understanding needed to confront these effects head-on, a display of youthful bravura could trap the mind in a quicksand of unresolved emotional needs or confusion. If this happens, the unresolved issues may work like a boa constrictor, squeezing out the life-force of the mind's new resolve, faith and spiritual energy.

This is why it is so important for the fledgling consciousness to spend time in meditation, dwelling in the inner worlds of silence and deep thought. In these silent worlds the mind's power and awareness grows, aided and supported by the loving consciousness of God.

Part 3

A Change of Mind

The vast power of the soul's spiritual universe is coiled deep within the mind's subconscious where it lies waiting to be activated. When the mind is aware, determined and focused it is able to freely access this spiritual life-force. And once these long sought-after powers are found and realized, they play an enormous role in reconstructing the framework of the spiritual mind.

Like a diver reaching into the depths to retrieve precious pearls from the ocean floor, the mind dives deep into the silent inner seas of its purest consciousness to embrace a new beginning, bringing to the surface of experience such wonders that can only revolutionize and transform the landscape of human consciousness.

The process of spiritual growth begins with a regular meditation practice and the unfolding of inner wisdom. Qualities and powers that have been long hidden by a lack of awareness and ignorance begin to surface in meditation, and become part of the mind's spiritual world. Through such experience of well-being and power, the mind slowly and gradually starts to transfer its allegiance from external influences and focus on its inner world as it begins to remember, recognize and nurture its subconscious.

With each inner journey and focused connection comes new awareness, new experience and new power. Each one becomes a facet of the soul's true heart. In this new, subtle orientation the old external patterns and formats of consciousness quickly lose strength, form and coherence. No longer supported or maintained by an active attitude and intention, they immediately start to weaken and disintegrate.

Step-by-step, like a reviving Atlantis, the spiritual mind slowly emerges to manifest its new form of beauty, power and sovereignty. At this time, like a protective mother, the soul's whole attention is centered on the support and development of its newly forming consciousness and remains constantly vigilant to the illusions and dangers of external influence and former old mindsets that lie in wait, ready to sabotage and abort its new life form.

As the mind leaves the old lands of confusion, it gradually becomes stronger, freer and more self-determining. It traverses the heady seas of awakening and change, and the beginning of this journey is supported solely by faith and theory. The mind is armed with nothing more than a new map of untried directions. And so it enters a transitional time in which the first steps are tentative and unsure. This transition is certainly not helped by the voices of its old world and connections, which may be strident in their opposition, skepticism and non-acceptance of its new path. So it's not surprising that the mind can begin to experience a cascade of questions, doubts and uncertainty.

Yet with all former illusions destroyed and former philosophical homelands burnt, where and to whom can the mind turn? Familiar storm clouds of distress and worry soon begin to loom and the boat of the new mind can enter stormy seas suddenly and find the going very difficult.

Even with its anchor of power, the mind is not strong enough to anchor itself within the harbor of the spiritual world. While its old nature and the world of multiple attractions still demand audience, only the company and the power of the Supreme can offer a sanctuary of respite, growth and reflection.

To facilitate a safe passage through this vulnerable and often turbulent period, the mind needs the support of like-minded travellers, but most of all it needs the guiding energy of the Supreme. Sheltered in the lea of God's great Tree and with His protective support, the nascent sapling of the spiritual mind can grow, develop and safely awaken to its spiritual truth.

Taking strength and support in the oasis of God's great love, the life-energy of spiritual knowledge can be experienced and assimilated more profoundly, deepening the soul's realization and connection with its essential form and nature. This infusion and experience awakens the mind's ancient spiritual memories, allowing it to re-establish its eternal, karmic relationship of love with the Supreme.

Once free of the entanglement and maze of its old thinking and mindset, and with enough power to disengage from its web of fears and attachments, the spiritual mind is imbued with subtlety and light and can ascend to the Supreme dimension of light and access God's vast, pure energy field.

Equipped with this new strength, the mind can relinquish its battle-scarred world of conflict and desires and with great joy and courage begin its journey into light. As the boat of true consciousness heads toward the long sought-for haven of happiness, the soul turns its back on sorrow-filled shores. It turns away from the citadels of its attachments and relationships, leaving the memories and scenarios of its accomplishments and many former roles. And as it does so, the lands of the old world begin to fade and are forgotten and the mind is pulled towards and absorbed into the power and wonder of the approaching world of God.

With the aid and guidance of the slowly divinizing intellect, imbued with knowledge, experience and determination, the unencumbered mind can move freely into the orbit and vibrational world of the Supreme and there is able to bring itself into direct focus and connection with the vast and unlimited mind of God. Like a loving brother, the intellect introduces the bridegroom of the mind to the love-center of God's great heart. The eternal lover finally meets its Beloved. And within that love-energy the soul is held, entranced and healed. The mind, so infused with this pure love, begins to deepen and embed its truth and spiritual heart, fixing it firmly within its eternal and original consciousness.

This God-conscious union dramatically accelerates spiritual change, awakening the intellect to deeper insight, awareness and wisdom, and exposing the mind to energies of unbelievable purity and power. The mind's connection with the Supreme acts like a generator, re-energizing the faint, flickering energies of the soul's diminishing strength as well as reanimating and reviving the fire and faith of the distant memories of spiritual belief. And with this, a great fountain of inner power is released into the channels of external consciousness and the old, tired world of the past is replaced by a world of beauty, vibrancy and freshness. A world fed by the new ascendant energy that flows freely from the sacred center of the soul's original form.

As this new spiritual world begins to manifest and settle within the framework of its subtle consciousness, the mind starts to harmonize – to reintegrate and reweave its scattered, disparate strands of harmony and wholeness back into the stillness and stability of its original and perfect form. In this process of unfolding and integration, in this resurrection of the mind and divinization of the intellect, the soul gradually reconstructs the perfect instrument for its manifestation. This discovery of the mind's original consciousness brings the rebirth of a lost world. It is the renaissance of being and, through the spiritual mind, the revelation of God's unique role.

The Pathway to Change

Just as the Moon travels on a celestial pathway to fullness, so the spiritual mind goes through set phases of development and refinement. As each mind state is developed – through meditation, reflection and by using newly developed virtues to interact in the outside world – the mind's vast spiritual consciousness and capacity first emerges and then deepens. It is like a lotus flower opening, with each new phase of empowerment and awareness manifesting through the light of application and the power of God's Consciousness. There are nine steps on this pathway to change, and this section of the book will guide you through each one in turn, with reflection and practical meditations:

1 The Clear Mind
Through spiritual knowledge and the experience of inner silence, the mind becomes free, cleansed and perceptive.

2 The Wisdom Mind
The revived and discerning intellect brings subtlety and depth to the newly clarified mind.

3 The Invisible Mind
Through reflection and silence the mind activates its inner powers and vibrational energies.

4 The Love Mind
The primal soul energy is accessed and becomes the guiding principle of consciousness.

5 The God-Centered Mind.
Once anchored in God's consciousness, the mind becomes protected, stable and empowered.

6 The Divine Mind
Consciousness becomes filled with spiritual truth and power.

7 The Angelic Mind
Working with subtle energies, the mind becomes a channel of light and spiritual strength, which is capable of linking the inner and outer worlds.

8 The God Knowing Mind
In its deepening relationship with the Supreme, the mind begins to know, see and experience deeper insights into the unlimited.

9 Future Mind
Finally, the consciousness finds true contentment and harmony.

1 The Clear Mind

The Clear Mind is like a lake: still, tranquil and in perfect, peaceful harmony. Even though the occasional circumstance may stroke the vast calmness of its mirrored world, the clear mind sits far beyond, anchored in its eternity and retaining a state of unclouded serenity. In its eternal, spiritual dimension of awareness it remains far beyond the influences and effects of the superficial world. Here nothing moves. All is as it was, deep and profound, a primordial cosmic energy, moving through, then beyond, physical form. Bringing change, but not changing, full, yet empty, playing its part within the great wheel of existence.

In the clear mind nothing old is kept and nothing old is recalled. There is no engagement with the process of accumulating pain, and there is nothing to weigh it down or trigger a reaction to its storerooms of fear and negative memory. For the clear mind there are no borders between past and future and no side scenes to entrap it and cause it to lose focus. There are no tormented dreams of what might have been and what could yet be. The clear mind is watchful and alert and remains within each golden, present moment. There is no deviation and no other way. Each scene is viewed and beheld in the beauty of its unfolding. For the clear mind there are no questions, no problems and no lingering doubts. Its open heart and intellect engage fully with the play of living forms, accepting the accuracy and uniqueness of each unfolding scene and role.

And from this emerges the joy of understanding and seeing the significance of each scene and sacred moment. The mind sings the anthem of happiness and dances to the music of oneness, realizing that it too is part of the divine play, an integral link in the rosary of universal harmony. It understands that each of us, each flower-formed soul, resembles petals drawn together to form the perfect flower of the perfect moment. And each interaction becomes a blueprint – the seed of the perfect flower garden of a perfect world.

With the clear mind illuminated by this light of self-awareness and seated in peace and mental tranquility, the old racing mind begins to slow and move into a more relaxed, reflective state. In this space of equanimity and insight a clarity of perception starts to develop that enables the mind not only to begin a deeper understanding of itself, but to develop greater awareness and empathy for other actors in life's great play.

Stepping back, the clear mind observes so many others struggling with their sense of identity, trying to the best of their abilities to interpret their parts and life's evolving scenes. Some are clear, some confused, some tired or angry. Some want answers and some just want out, but most are totally oblivious of the great play of life that circles them. They are like children in a playground, completely preoccupied with their own games. They have become lost in the issues and tensions of emotions and lost in the wild throng of hurt and hearsay. All are separated from reality, trapped in the prisons of their needs and fears. Some may call for help, some for home, some for answers, while all around the songs of the children ring out with fervent pleas of "why?" and "what?", "how?" and "who?". These pleas join to become part of an anthem, deviously created and conducted by the two great illusionists: 'I' and 'Mine'. It is a masterpiece, a symphony of pain.

Beholding this jumbled jigsaw of colliding parts, the clear mind becomes aware that each soul – each actor on life's great stage – is dealing with the repercussions of their individual past. Each is striving towards their own conception of truth, beauty and natural order, trying everything they can to experience an idealized, personal world. Yet all are often heavily influenced by the weight of wrong awareness and the pull of wrong choice.

With this new awareness, the clear mind is filled with compassion, good will and understanding for every soul trapped in the seeming madhouse of myriad choices and so-called realities. Three steps are needed to maintain the clear mirror of perceptivity: closeness, cleanliness and clarity:

Step 1 Closeness
Firstly it is necessary to be close to the Supreme, the central source of spiritual consciousness and power. The physical plane, with its rapidly diminishing energy fields, is increasingly unable to provide a stable, sustaining foundation for the soul's endeavors. In God's oasis of support the mind can grow. The clear mind is held secure in the nurturing and regenerating bastion of God's pure heart, even as the spinning vortex of the deteriorating lower fields try to pull energy into their downward spiral.

Step 2 Cleanliness
The cleansing process works in three ways:

A) When a light is shone into the darkest recesses of a long-unused room, dust and rubbish appear. In the same way, when the mind opens its consciousness to God's pure and powerful radiance, negative attitudes and untrue beliefs are soon unmasked. In front of God's clear light these illusions and false structures rapidly lose power and credibility. They begin to disintegrate.

B) The vast, unlimited, pure light-energy of the Supreme acts like a filter, washing and dissolving the crumbling remnants of the mind's old nature.

C) Cleansing is finally accomplished when the intellect consciously allows and directs spiritual energy into the soul's experiential world. The intellect frees the soul's core nature, allowing it to manifest like a flowing fountain, refreshing and re-energizing the riverbed of the inner-self to reveal a pure pristine world.

Step 3 Clarity
As the mind becomes aware, it is able to drop the veils of external

forms and their mazes of convoluted pathways and link instead directly to the essential significance of each scene and intention. Motives, feelings and influences become clear. The mind moves into knowing and responds accordingly.

No longer bullied, threatened or trapped by fears, indecision and wrong judgments, the clear mind sits on the crest of a cloud in detachment and lightness. Finally it has become the arbiter of its own choices and knows the consequences of its thoughts and actions. Thus, it makes the right responses and the right actions, triggering an upward spiral of positivity and positive effects. As a result, life becomes one of contentment and success.

Practical ways to use the Clear Mind:

- Start each new day and interaction by dipping your mind into the cleansing waters of inner silence to eradicate the effects of any previous influences.
- Then imagine that your mind is standing on a balcony of awareness, so you become a spectator previewing and assessing the scenes around you.
- Remind yourself that satisfaction and positive outcomes happen when youare both authentic, totally centered in your own truth, and filled with pure feelings of good wishes and benevolence for everyone.
- Maintain an awareness that behind every action, regardless of the plan or intended outcome, there is always a nobler objective or higher design. So keep searching for, and working towards, that goal.

Let us sit in silence and reflect for a moment on what it is to achieve a clear mind, repeating these thoughts:

Meditation

"Around me the air is soft and still.
Branches and boughs reach out into a timeless world,

where large fronded leaves, motionless and perfectly poised,
are held as if in an eternal trance.
Then a ripple, a breeze,
and all nature moves with one accord –
to nod and sway their unified ascent
and then return
to harmony,
to the sacred order
that is nature's way.
And I, too, learn from this,
to be who I am.
To understand that contentment and well-being
come from stillness.
And that each one has their role, their part,
that all are trying to manifest their truth,
meeting and responding as best they can
to the deep inner pulls of the spiritual self.
And I acknowledge and respect this.
And now I focus on what I need to do.
On what I must do.
For I now realize
it's time to walk the path of my inner truth,
to listen to the call of my spiritual heart
and in the silence of my focused mind
to allow the light of God's pure light
to give me strength and hope and sight,
that I may see and grasp
the precious jewels of eternal truth;
to use and guide and find
the inner sanctuary,
the sacred center of my soul.
And then to draw deep on
the powers of natural love
and natural law;

healing and freeing me
from the patterns of old reaction,
from the hurts of numerous sorrows.
With my mind now free
and light and clear,
like a bird,
I now begin to fly."

2 The Wisdom Mind

Like a floating lotus, the wisdom mind sits in stillness. With tranquility of thought, minutely observing, but not setting up a platform for the observed to materialize its effect. It understands that behind each façade lies a deeper well of meaning and knows that each step – each turning scene – reveals some new wisdom. So, with reflective thought, the wisdom mind opens and frees the significance that lies in all things. And these become stepping stones, helping it to cross the great river of illusion and so transforming into jewels of learning, insight and new avenues for further, deeper experience.

The wisdom mind has a great treasury of insight. A major aspect of this is the way it unravels the inner secrets of knowledge and understands their pertinence to practical life. In order to do so, the wisdom mind explores and traverses three levels of spiritual depth:

Level 1 Surface
Firstly the wisdom mind explores the immediate surface form – this is the initial gateway to that particular truth – and explains and clarifies former unawareness or confusion. The processes and systems that we formerly followed, often with no real understanding, are now either abandoned or overlaid by a consciousness that is guided by spiritual intelligence.

Level 2 Outer World
The second level of spiritual depth explored by the wisdom mind looks at the outer personal world of the researcher. By offering greater meaning and relevance, the wisdom mind embeds its truth within the receptive consciousness.

Level 3 Universality
The third level of insight concerns universality, or the interconnectedness of the entire spectrum of spiritual truth. Each truth, like a glittering jewel, quickly reveals its position in the cosmos of eternal wisdom and each truth, once rediscovered and applied, becomes a building block in the restoration of a harmonious universe. The mind enters the unlimited.

Because it possesses the tools of the discerning intellect, the wisdom mind enters a vast, fertile, hinterland of extended knowledge. Like a grappling octopus it takes hold of tenets of truth and pulls them below the surface of meaning, and in that subtle expanse starts to draw out significances, implications and connections.

Each moment and each movement of this divine inner dance resembles a new-blossoming flower. As each petal opens, new treasures are offered up, revealing the profundity, delight and the immense power of the constantly expanding landscape of spiritual awareness. It causes the mind to whirl and sing as if filled with the helium of euphoria and the intoxication of knowing. And thus, having answered all questions, the mind moves into wisdom.

The path of the wisdom mind is narrow and steep, yet at the same time spacious, open and, most importantly, clear. But a path that is littered with the casualties of distraction, those trapped in a cocoon of their ego's needs. There are many former wisdom searchers who have become like marooned ships, drawn onto the rocks, distracted by the momentary lure and appeal of the illusory worlds; stranded with no direction or bearing. Yet, unwilling or unable to acknowledge their error, with a false bravura they play out their game. However, behind the façade they become like beggars, bargaining and beseeching, offering and praying, lost in the tumult of despair and hoping that solutions and happiness will again somehow just suddenly appear.

Spiritual inner power works like a cube of raw jelly that has to be freed from its packet, then softened and liquefied before being poured into a mold. Within this solid framework, the newly active mind gradually reformulates and sets to establish a new energy of strength and protection.

The externally driven ego-mind, concerned primarily with being clever and performing its words, remains on the outer surface of this power. It shuns and ignores any inner stance, treating it as if it were a threat that would prevent it from sharing the limelight of the moment. Yet when the tsunamis of negative influences come rushing to the shore, the ego-driven mind, having no sanctuary or strength, is quickly swamped and overcome. And the artifices of its seemingly spiritual cleverness are not enough protection from these storms.

The wisdom mind knows what it has to keep and what it has to give. It keeps careful counsel, knowing that the secret of each moment unfolds in numerous ways and through numerous forms. Like the crane, which waits with patient stealth as it hunts, the mind also waits, discerning the moment of engagement. Then it strikes, acting with power, love and gentle words.

The law of return ensures that what is given is returned equally, and then more. The giver experiences not only the flow and support of the returning empowerment, but also subtle blessings and gratitude from the recipients. The wisdom mind, understanding the law of accumulation and return, knows that it has to give away all that it has received. Reflection and meditation bring the soul's inherent treasures to the forefront, but their true value and sparkle come when the treasures of the inner world are used to illuminate and restore the fallen worlds of others.

Spiritual power is initially inert and dormant until used in the process of benevolence. Then, as in the story of Aladdin's genie, through the act of giving, this great power and potential becomes active and alive and a force for change and transformation.

The wisdom mind knows that the storms and difficulties that come from individuals, situations and circumstances of the world are all illusory. They are the things of the physical world and its world is of the spiritual. It understands that when others bring disturbances and trials they are not to be blamed, since they act without will or wisdom. They are victims of illusion and misunderstanding who have been trapped and are hypnotized by the prevailing influences and negative effects of their past interactions.

The wisdom mind knows that whatever seed it sows will bear fruit. It waits with awareness and patience, knowing that the fruit of positive action may come quickly or come according to the season. So, the wisdom mind's attention and focus is on the quality of the seed and the preparation of the land. It knows that only through love will things change, and only through love will things work, and only through love will it be satisfied and fulfilled. So love is the only path it walks. The wisdom mind learns to see only itself and through this it learns to see God and through seeing God, it then can see others. So, in listening, watching and waiting, the wisdom mind accepts the scene before it and then with subtlety, empathy and careful compassion it unwraps the outer covering to gradually reveal the true intention found inside and then works toward a harmonious outcome.

For the wisdom mind, the path of purpose and direction is a continuous one. It is a journey of learning, observation and transformation. It is about questioning everything, yet also accepting without doubt, fear or self-elevation. The wisdom mind thinks lightly, but takes nothing lightly. It travels and moves, yet always remains still, centered within each moment. The wisdom mind knows that only through inner power can the challenges of the journey be accomplished and so it works entirely in this world of subtlety and silence.

Practical ways to use the Wisdom Mind:
- Reflect every day on life's continuously unfolding drama.
- Recognize that often what is happening and what is said are not always what are intended.
- Remember that subterfuge, camouflage or inner confusion can manifest easily.
- Ask whether subterfuge and confusion are being used to hide a fear of rejection or of being derided rather than being deceitful.
- The wisdom mind sees each one's heart and true intentions and so goes beyond the words, goes beyond the actions to embrace each one's intrinsic goodness.
- The wisdom mind understands that each one comes with a particular wisdom, so always thinks: what have they come to teach me?

Let us sit in silence and reflect for a moment on the wisdom mind, repeating these thoughts:

In all things there is the good.
In each, the jewel of the good
awaits to emerge.
In every action and
In every circumstance
there is the good.
I see it and understand
With the eye of peace and patience,
for in all things

there is the good.
Let me stand back,
think less and be still
so my vision fills
with understanding and
my heart fills with mercy.
For in all things there is the good.
For too often the veil of illusion
of outer form
clouds the good.
Let me stand back
think less and be still.
I change the pattern of my response.
I see the benefit, the beauty,
the way for me ahead.
For in all things
there is the good.

3 The Invisible Mind

Like a warm wind brushing a tear-stained cheek, the invisible mind flows within us, embracing the scenes of present need. Subtle thoughts do not simply synthesize and resolve the quandaries of a perplexed mind, they are also vehicles of vibrational and subtle support. Empowered and protected in the dimension of silence, the spiritual mind is strengthened and becomes resilient against the mixed energy flows surrounding its world. It is able to maintain a concentrated focus of compassionate thought and channel it directly to the place of need without breaking apart or being deviated by the influence of another chain of thoughts.

The invisible mind generates its intention through a sustained experience of meditation. From that place of silence, there emerges a deep and pure desire to give support or love to those in particular states of need or distress. This is part of the mind's evolving spiritual nature. These thoughts are channeled from the mind's heart center and travel on the energy vibration of pure compassion. Although the surrounding energy fields are negative and disturbed, they are weak in comparison and so are unable to absorb or deflect this flow and vibration. On reaching their intended focus these thoughts are received as either a rush of new, positive energy, or manifest as a subtle form of thought that brings feelings of assurance, support and even guidance.

The act of supporting others through difficulties can be greatly inhibited when we encounter individual egos, inner blocks, mental confusion and physical distance. Yet the invisible mind overcomes such things as it begins to work from its deep soul center, aligning and combining its consciousness with the pure energies of the Supreme. Pure and subtly directed thought can break through the low frequency or negative energy barriers that often prevail in the auras of others and in the heavy atmospheres surrounding us.

Filled and directed by love, the invisible mind's pure vibrational energies are drawn to and connect with the individual's own heart center, which allows them to bypass any blocks of fear and ego. These subtle, yet powerful thoughts immediately act as a catalyst of change, injecting the individual with spiritual power and stimulating his or her inner energies. A process of positive revitalization and healing is set in motion, working simultaneously on all the individual's energy bodies. This input of power and energy equips the individual to move into a more positive space and to set about creating a more self-determined and fulfilling lifestyle.

Through this subtle work, the invisible mind releases positive energies that act like an incense stick on the prevailing atmosphere, transforming each connecting frequency-field as they experience the impact of the channeled power. These spiritually pure vibrations of love and peace change the energy flows. Things start to shift and move. The heavy and negative psychic clouds that had formerly settled over individuals and events are lifted and things seem lighter and brighter. In fact, these vibrational waves continue to travel outwards, going on to influence and affect the surrounding worlds of matter, nature and the animal kingdom.

To sustain a spiritual consciousness at this level, the mind needs to develop a high degree of purity in its focus, attention and attitude. The energy frequencies are such that the mind must be empty of all negative and disturbing influences, which are extremely counter-productive to any form of subtle working. A deep, silent experience produces the necessary power and platform for the mind to free itself of any of these impure effects. The invisible mind is then able to direct its thoughts and vibrations with a strong and determined focus to wherever it is needed.

Practical ways to use the Invisible Mind:

- The spiritual mind changes atmospheres through pure vibration. So, start the day by filling the room of the mind with an atmosphere of positivity and enthusiasm.
- Before you interact with others, send a thought-vibration of powerful energy to your destination to create an environment of peaceful coexistence and cooperation.
- Travel with an aura of peace around you. This acts as protection, disabling potential threats caused by anger or ego; such energy says "welcome" to peace, and to any confrontation it says "depart".
- If people come to you full of confusion and sorrow, help lift their heaviness by surrounding and supporting them with peaceful compassion, allowing them space for respite and reconciliation.

Let us sit in silence now and reflect for a moment on the invisible mind, by repeating these thoughts:

Meditation

I see around me
a world of tears
and pain
and great sadness
where brothers fight
and inflict injustice.
The family of mankind
now lies wounded
on the field of sorrow
and Mother Earth
bends her head in grief.
Yet, now from its
center of love –
the center of light –
the soul opens
its heart center
and emerges
compassion and mercy
and the purest feelings of goodwill.
Centered in that globe,
in that arc of purest consciousness,
I send pure thoughts
of pure vibration,
of purest love,
to touch all hearts,
all minds,
for this is the energy –
the power of true feelings.
It is the light of healing,
it is the light of peace
and hope
and reconciliation,
enabling all to forgive

and to forget
and to resolve all that has occurred.
And the light that is sent –
it fills the darkness.
In that light,
all can see
and all can feel
the reality,
the way of true being,
of true brotherhood.

4 The Love Mind

Like the warm sun flooding the earth's fragrant flowers with its gentle light of life, the love mind spreads vibrations of good wishes and pure feelings of well-being to all. And like the waves of the deep ocean that gently caress the curving beach, the loving mind shares and cooperates, then lets go. Just as the honeybee is obsessively devoted to each flower, the love mind gives undivided focus and respect to each and every soul. It is like the rain cloud, full and effusive, bringing freshness and life to the tired, dry land – in such a way the love mind brings an atmosphere of kindness, enthusiasm and new hope. And like the caring mother with her demanding child, the love mind places each soul in the center of its pure and high regard.

But just as water flows through different lands, accumulating influences and debris on its journey to the sea, so too the love-needy mind is continuously contaminated and influenced by external effects as it travels through the physical world. The more the mind tries to resurrect the world of love, the more it becomes entangled, confused in debate with its physical form and related connections. And over time, slowly and gradually, the shimmering love, light and energy of the soul dims and falls into the shadow worlds of forgetfulness and unknowing.

With knowledge of the spiritual self and the gradual

movement away from influence, it becomes easier and more natural for the spiritual mind to move into love. Employing the spiritual intellect, the empowered mind is able to travel deep into its heart center of spiritual power, where it can begin to explore and mine the sacred treasures of its inner world. As the dust of disuse is swept away, a precious, love-faceted form of ancient beauty is revealed. It is a form so long hidden and so long sought. It is the pristine and perfect form of the soul's pure love center.

This love, that has been so long dormant, stirs and flickers into recognition, spreading its warmth and new life through the corridors and portals of the mind, opening and discovering the long-locked chambers of the subtle self. With guidance, and the careful management of thoughts and interactions, the flame of love develops and asserts its influence throughout the super-structure of the mind.

Yet it is not until the intellect brings this reviving love into the immense energy-flow of the Supreme that the heart energy of love is truly ignited. Then it becomes a force – an intense furnace of unlimited and active love. Love-fed, love-filled and love-centered, the spiritual mind is held in this resurgent arena of vibrant consciousness.

Having found the thing it had so long searched for, the mind can no longer be held to ransom, or be deceived by false and empty promises. For it has been reunited with the Holy Grail of all its desires, the central love-jewel of its own pure heart. And so, in this way, the world changes.

Like a flower held in the embrace of the soft, warming sun, like nature swayed by the charm and magic of a summer's day, the love mind becomes enveloped in the spell of pure, subtle love. Within this spell there are no questions, no projections and no desires; there is no pain. There is only an exquisite feeling of well-being and harmony – consciousness opens up and accepts and embraces all existence. The heart becomes a channel, a source of pervasive, universal love that flows like a gentle sea over all things. And in the heart-center of the mind there is a feeling of total love.

Within this love consciousness, the mind can see the unfolding scenes of the great dramatic play of the world and begin to understand that all is well and as it should be. Nothing is wrong or out of place, there is just the eternal flow of energy that shapes, expands, moves, disperses and re-forms again according to the formulations of consciousness. And whether consciousness is limited and narrow or unlimited and full, the love mind sees, accepts and understands.

When the mind is destabilized and stressed by the proliferation of choice and direction and is brainwashed and infected by needs and desires, the heart becomes trapped and tortured in the high-walled prisons of selfishness and fear. Yet for the love mind there are no desires to compete and possess. It has finished its infatuation and dance with materialism. It has seen through the futility of a life reliant on money and status. It has finished with the anger and frustrations that come from attempting to organize the lives of others. It has dismounted from its high horse of self-promoting opinions and finally stopped all its jousting with the windmills of illusion. Centered within the fragrant, fertile garden of its inner world, experiencing the joy of its unfolding, and tended and nurtured by the caring, shaping hands of the Supreme Great Gardner, the love mind is at rest.

In this sanctuary of compassion, the love mind becomes a haven of calm to the storm-tossed souls of the world. For in their frantic concern for money, possessions and acclaim they are swept far out into the heaving seas of endless desire, where wave upon wave of need and fear, incessant and unbearable, constantly breaks upon their fragile minds.

In its serene waters of spiritual peace, the love mind offers a garden of respite and an alternative direction to the beleaguered travellers of the troubled way. Through lifestyle and example, through vibration and attitude, through company and power, it becomes a lighthouse. This beacon is a touchstone and a mirror that ignites and triggers the dormant love energies of those around it. Its vibrations and powers breech the precipitous walls of ego and fear, empowering wandering souls to flee the confines of their incarceration and awaken to their inner truth and onward journey.

Practical ways to use the Love Mind:
- When meeting others, be aware that regardless of the attitude and the approach they may take, each one desires the highest positive outcome and each one is trying to ascend to the summit of their ideals.
- Though you may have a different viewpoint and response to anotherperson, honor his or her views and actions. Listen, appreciate and support others' intentions with positive regard and respect.
- Remember that through such acceptance and support we begin to weave together the strands of unity and true friendship. By seeing and knowing each other in this way we sow the seeds of love.
- Let no one leave me without some inner benevolence or positive support.

Let us sit in silence now and reflect for a moment, experiencing the consciousness of the loving mind by repeating these thoughts:

Meditation
"In my inner world
my mind is still and peaceful,
supported by a flowing fountain of soft, gentle love.
This love issues from the center
of my pure, spiritual heart.

It is a love that surrounds and protects
and guides each thought, each action.
And there, the effects of the past
and the influences of the world
cannot intrude,
cannot come to disrupt the serene and tranquil state
that overlays and fills my heart.
And so, entranced in this present moment
and in this stillness and in this love,
I am now open and receptive to God's pure love,
which begins to lift and transform my love
into a vibrant, resonating
world of active compassion.
And this love that now moves out,
beyond.
It touches all souls
and all hearts.
This love is completely accepting,
unifying,
inspiring.
Its energy reminds, awakens and draws
all souls to their own unique love,
to their own true heart,
to their own true self."

5 The God-Centered Mind

Over a period of time the mind experiences and develops a susceptibility to influence, particularly to the ideas and the nature of others. It also has a huge dependency on the support facilities of the material world. For the freedom-loving mind, these become prisons of support. When the mind loses its awareness and ability to help itself, it quickly becomes lost, trapped in the ever-changing shadow worlds of superficial personality, external glamour and the entangling web of technological need.

Thus shackled, the mind finds itself in a continual state of desire and disempowerment. Left to limp along in the twilight world of non-achievement, it becomes a spiritual dwarf, deprived of the sunlight of its own achievements and spiritual beauty. Reduced to living off the crumbs of superficial achievement and praise, with the forlorn hope of a miraculous intervention, the soul is left like a shipwrecked sailor, lost and abandoned, searching and calling, desperate for rescue. The memory of what formerly was may have faded, causing the mind's former world of spiritual beauty and its relationship with the Supreme to slip away. Although for many, this may be a vague, distant memory, for most it is simply forgotten.

Lost and locked in a befuddled amnesia and full of discontent and sorrow, the mind may find itself wandering among the islands and wastelands of various false Gods with their confused philosophies and fervent promises, calling for some sort of help. It is wishing and promising and hoping beyond hope to return to an idealized, yet unclear state of well-being.

Yet among all the confusion, sorrows and deceptions, and among the myriad rites and rituals, the mind still carries a flickering subconscious faith that all could be well; that a reunion with truth and the world of harmony is still possible.

But there may be countless false dawns, betrayals and spiritual cul-de-sacs. In an anguish of spiritual despair, the mind repudiates all blame and shakes its metaphorical fist directly at God and the world of spiritual truth. Embittered and angry, the mind fervently disowns and denounces its old, long-time Beloved, like a cast-off lover. It conveniently forgets that it once believed, accepted and was beguiled by the sweet-worded promises and deceits of those who claimed to speak for God. It was the mind itself that chose to fall for the charms of a multitude of other dalliances. With this rejection and denial of God, the mind's separation from truth was complete.

Yet though it may be faint and flickering, the flame of spiritual truth is never totally extinguished. And from time to time when it comes in contact with the vibrations and actions of kindness, truth and spiritual love, the sleeping inner heart stirs and opens its rimy lids, allowing love's memory to slowly splutter into being. On that wave of awakening and resurgent love, the recollection of a former ancient love returns. It is a memory etched deep into the soul's eternal mind, the memory of its first true relationship and true love: the memory of a relationship with God.

As the God-centered mind allows these feelings to take hold and starts to believe in the ephemeral and intriguing butterfly of a lost and idealized love, it remembers the hidden pathway to the oasis of God's sacred heart. With this recollection the mind's inner archive begins to awaken. Hidden among its great sacred truths and rediscovered jewels is the memory, experience and path into God's divine world. And it is with recognition and joy that the spiritual mind enters the energy field of God.

Focused in the love center of God's pure light and detached from the energies of physical form and the material world, the mind is able to concentrate its awareness on the Supreme. Seated in the most perfect consciousness, the Supreme mind is one that is completely egoless, benevolent and pure, and its unlimited love welcomes the love-thirsty soul. Feeling reassured and safe, the mind opens its long-hidden heart to the pure, unconditional heart of God. It is a meeting of eternal forms. It is a union of pure light energies. It is the meeting of the spiritual family – the eternal parent and the returning child. It is the end of night and the dawn of life.

Having struggled with and puzzled over the reality of its truth for so long, on discovering this union, the mind experiences an explosion of realization and pure consciousness. The Supreme's unlimited energy engulfs the soul, triggering an experience of metamorphosis – of incredible absorption, healing and becoming. It is the butterfly awakening and breaking free of the cocoon of inner debate, moving into the clear light of knowing, into the clear sky of experience.

In the unity of light and silence within the depths of Supreme love, the old external and negative nature that the mind nurtured for so long begins to fade, being replaced by a new paradigm and a new pattern of spiritual consciousness.

This quickly brings change and a new form appears. For as the God-centered mind shimmers in the embrace of this supernal light, it starts to lose the shape and structure that held it together throughout its initial spiritual awakening. As the mind's spiritual qualities, powers and identity begin to develop, it suddenly understands the meaning of the separation of soul and body and gradually the separate parts of its new form start to transform.

As God's unbounded love-energy pulls the soul into the experience of complete pure consciousness, the mind discovers an unlimited dimension: it has no boundaries, no limits and no sense of depth, width or capacity. Here there is no connection to analogy and no comparisons or contrasts; the mind simply experiences the world of truth. In this unlimited domain of Supreme, spiritual consciousness the mind is absorbed in a mesmeric field of incredible power and harmonic unity. Just like two long-lost lovers whose souls come together with one thought and one experience, the mind moves into unity and love.

Through spiritual knowledge the mind enters a world of awareness and through its connection with God it enters a world of power. It shifts into a new dimension. And through this restoration of the divine trinity of spiritual knowledge, soul and God, the mind awakens from its dream and the illusory world of the past is no more. Here, its old nature loses prominence and power, relinquishing its sovereignty to that of spiritual divinity and Godly love. This becoming – this transformation – is overseen and nurtured by the care and compassion of the Supreme, whose love provides a canopy of protection and a field of reflective learning that equips the mind to move into empowerment and full consciousness.

From such a vantage point of illumination, former issues, traumas and sorrows become like paper tigers and huge mountains of fear and worry seem as small as mustard seeds and as insignificant as cotton wool. For through the combined form of mind and Supreme Mind, the old adversaries of inner conflict and fear are understood and vanquished, absorbed into the acceptance and oneness of the world of unlimited love.

Practical ways to use the God-Centered Mind:

- When confronted by the upheavals and storms of loss, health and relationship, position your consciousness in God's sacred center and experience the great peaceful stillness, clarity, support and healing.
- Although there may be tumult and turmoil all around you, stay cocooned in this energy field of protective love.
- Whatever situations are thrown up, whatever specters come knocking at your door, simply step into God's unlimited world and draw respite, strength and new resolve.

Let us sit in silence and reflect for a moment, considering the God-centered mind by repeating these thoughts:

Meditation
I turn my thoughts away
From the cares and actions of the day.
As I enter into the realm of silence,
I become focused on my inner qualities
Of light and love and peace.
My mind becomes still, calm and free.
In this calmness and light
I can let go of my physical identity

and the things of the world,
and I travel to a state beyond the cosmos,
to a region of purest light and complete silence.
Here I make contact with the purest energy,
the light of the supreme consciousness,
the Supreme Soul.
As I enter into this light,
my thoughts and feelings are held
by that pure love-light energy.
I am absorbed into
that power,
that radiant energy,
which surrounds
and comforts me.
And I stay centered in this light,
experiencing,
becoming light.
And in this orb of spiritual light,
I feel myself being healed,
recharged,
rejuvenated
and cleansed.
The sorrows and influences of the past
and the effects of old habits diminish and fall away.
I experience being fulfilled and satisfied,
Full of light and love and peace.

6 The Divine Mind

Far beyond the lower worlds, far beyond the great seas of turbulent emotion and far beyond the ever-changing scenes of the world's great play, the divine mind sits on the throne of awareness, illuminated by its inner light, empowered by love and motivated by compassion. From here, it watches, it sees and it understands.

When the mind is no longer linked to causal law and to the ambivalent flows of the material plane, it finds another purpose and focus. Disengaged from the constraints of physical form and from the limited play of life's ongoing drama, the mind's freed consciousness is able to connect with and tune into the energy of the Supreme. In this sacred communion and confluence of spiritual energies, the vast influence of the Supreme's huge energy field dramatically affects the mind's spiritual DNA, altering its vibrational frequency and structure. Formed over time by desire, fear and a self-centered ego, the separated and fragmented parts of the mind start to break apart and refor-mulate to match the unlimited mind of the Supreme and move into alignment with His clear, pure consciousness. In this way the fragmented mind becomes whole. It is two energies and two minds that, though separate, are combined. It is two minds becoming as one.

As the mind thinks about God, even without realizing, it moves into an aspect of the unlimited. The karma of love immedi-ately draws the mind into the energy field of God's open heart. And the searching mind receives refreshment, encouragement and power to help it venture further into the vast cosmos of this divine world. In this arena of realization, the mind is able to see, know and recognize that which was formerly hidden, blocked by the wrong choices of its past. Once free of the old influences, the nature and power of God's reality become evident and accessible.

The mind of God is found in silence. The mind of God communicates through silence. In this vast pure mind there is no expansion of thought, no connectivity of ideas, no projection of emotion. It is an intellect that holds everything, yet is completely empty and free, an awareness that is complete and absolute and a knowing that needs no reflection or acknowledgement. The mind of God is a sacred consciousness of truth and absolute love that is totally absorbed in bliss. And the newly awakened divine mind opens to this understanding and experience.

Just like an awakening flower is pulled by the rays of the ascendant sun, the divine mind of the soul opens and becomes receptive to this ancient power. The soul's subtle heart responds and revives, moving into full consciousness where it begins to recall and remember its original, but forgotten, transcendent relationship with the Supreme. And with each new experience a desire to slip the leash of the body and the influence of the lower worlds and move into the orbit of God's wonderful world grows within the mind.

As when the night yields to the power of the coming day, the mind is drawn into the vibrant, revitalizing and long-sought energy of God's welcoming love. Even here this love is difficult to maintain as the remnants of the old nature and the pulls of an impure world work to disengage the mind. But as its personal purity and relationship with the Supreme increases and deepens, the mind finally becomes able to firmly hold its focus and connection. And the more it allows itself to be pulled into silence, the stronger and more powerful it is able to resist external influences. Thus each experience – each step – becomes a transformation. It is a metamorphosis through the continuing journey into ascendancy: the caterpillar, the chrysalis and the butterfly.

It is the touchstone power of the Supreme that dramatically draws the soul into the pure globe of divine experience, ushering in the emergence and manifestation of the complete divine mind. A mind succored at the wellspring of eternal power; a mind created in the heart center of God's pure love. And in that cocoon of purest love, the effects and the debris of wrong consciousness begin to lose their hold and are superseded by spiritual wisdom and an influx of spiritual power.

At this point a new love and a new consciousness emerge, and become the religion and ruler of the heart. And in this experience of divine love, the mind becomes completely freed, aware and linked intrinsically to essential truth and the unity of God's unlimited and universal heart.

For the divine mind, understanding is united with internal experience and change. Duality and fragmentation of thought and attitude are no more. Once its spiritual eye of awareness has opened, restoring original vision, the divine mind is able clearly to see its beauty, its purpose and the true way of right action.

With that clarity, the missing pieces of truth's jigsaw are found, placed and completed, thus awakening a universal consciousness – a restoration and reunion with the spiritual world family. Being aware of the connectedness of all philosophical and belief systems, the mind's struggles with rejection are replaced by an emerging love that embraces all with its unlimited acceptance and deep understanding.

Seated in the tower of God's loving consciousness, the divine mind, with its new, expansive vision clearly sees the essence of the great world play – its energy fields, forms, movements and formulations. It sees that all energy is malleable, all energy is subject to synchronicity, all energy changes through pure thought and that all is harmonized through pure love.

In this state of stability and stillness, at the hub and pivot of the three eternal worlds of God, matter and the self, the divine mind becomes both the instigator and orchestrator of change. It draws power from the Supreme and feeds it into the lifeblood of its own consciousness, which then transmits those vibrations into the energy fields of the world. The mind draws inspiration, learning and virtue from the physical world and returns vibrations of appreciation and a deep bonded love. Emerging from within itself, the divine mind finds the wisdom of experience and shares it with others.

Gone is the despair and the reactions to the often confusing and chaotic play of life. Gone are attempts to change and reorder another's role, or another's way. Gone is the beseeching and imploring to higher worlds for interventions and gone, finally, is the self's proud, pompous self-opinionated solutions to the so-called failings of world systems and the collapse of individual ideals and responses.

Having reunited and reasserted its role and relationship in the great circle of eternal energy, the divine mind becomes like the Norse Rainbow Bridge: a link connecting the Creator and the creation, a new channel that ensures the flow and renewal of pure and active energy.

The divine mind is clear in what it needs to do, what it has to do and what it wants to do. It moves to become the cipher, the outlet of new consciousness. It is like a philosopher's stone that triggers the sleeping wisdom and long-forgotten memories of each one's inner world and plants the seed of energy, healing and renewal in the flower gardens of the world.

Practical ways to use the Divine Mind:

- Remember that you have only to enter the wisdom world of God's clear mind to move into awareness.
- Always distance yourself from misunderstanding and misinterpretation. Simply watch, observe and remain full of love.
- As you look around try to see the many differences and divisions as separated branches of the same world family tree. So too life and death are a harmonious continuum, a dance of change and renewal.
- Be aware that both the haves and the have-nots reap what they have sown in the tidal flow of the ocean of karmic interaction.

Let us sit in silence and reflect for a moment, considering the divine mind and repeating the following thoughts:

Meditation

I am the soul,
I am the observer.
I watch and see

the actors and the actions,
the comings and goings;
who moves and uses,
and shares and takes.
I am the observer,
I am detached.
My subtle, soul light form
sees, holds,
but does not need;
is not dependent
on the forms, the structures, the circumstances
of the material plane.
I see the expectations, the confusions,
the colliding parts,
yet, I stand back, detached,
knowing that each one is the shaper,
the creator,
the reconciler of their part.
I stand back,
hold back,
full of love.
I cannot play their part
or change the scenes.
But in my state of self awareness,
linked to the restorative center
of God's great light,
I can give support and strength
and send that light,
to guide,
to inspire,
to help move the illusion,
so that all can dance
and all can sing
and fly to the world of light.

7 The Angelic Mind

The angelic mind is a translucent, iridescent and beautiful jewel through which the light of God's pure consciousness and eternal light flows from the cosmic world. During its journey of enlightenment, the angelic mind is dramatically transformed through its relationship with the Supreme. It moves into a world of pure unlimited love. A love that is ancient, a love nurtured through long ages of spiritual time, a love long forgotten, but now revived, drawn from the deep heart-center of the eternal soul. This love is so powerful and intense that the mind abandons its attachments, its self-obsession and its old ego forms of 'I' and 'Mine'. All fall away and seem irrelevant, insignificant and pointless beside the immense sun of God's unlimited world.

And thus it is in God's great heart that the angelic mind finally accomplishes its epic journey of long millennia: the long-sought dream to reach the lands of eternal truth and taste the eternal love of the Great Beloved. There it is embraced and drawn deep into the haven of God's heart-world and like the sun-centered rose, the mind becomes consumed, absorbed and intoxicated in the tumult of this pure and wondrous experience of unlimited love.

Empty of desire, deceit and self-centeredness, the angelic mind, embodied with truth and pure consciousness, becomes worthy and able to hold onto and share the sacred truths of spiritual wisdom that were previously lost, dismissed from relevance by the impure and ego-conscious physical mind. It becomes guardian, gatekeeper and trustee to these inner worlds, allowing access only to those hearts with true and pure intent.

As gatekeeper to the sacred worlds, the angelic mind awakens and draws the seeker-soul to the doorways of new consciousness. Its consciousness is a beacon of light that alerts those who are lost and searching, bringing them to the portal of awareness. There are three doorways at the crossing point to this new freedom:

Doorway 1: The Doorway of Truth

The seeking mind is given a mirror that reflects its true form, qualities, powers and special beauty. It is shown laws of action and interaction and its relationship with time. In accepting and experiencing this, the mind steps through the doorway. On stepping through, it sheds the falsehoods of the physical world and adopts the costume of the soul. In this form and alignment, the mind once again becomes its own truth. In the court of this new ruler of the inner ways, any external thinking and projection that previously divorced the mind from its true consciousness has no more influence.

Doorway 2: The Doorway to God

Having discovered spiritual self-awareness, the mind is introduced to the form, nature and experience of the Supreme. In recognizing and accepting the reality of God's pure form and elevated consciousness, the mind passes through a doorway into the dimension of God's pure world and the world of relationship between the soul and the Supreme Soul. It is a realm of awakening, understanding and deep spiritual insight – a dimension of love, acceptance, healing and power.

Doorway 3: The Doorway to the Future Worlds

Through applied consciousness, the travelling mind gains a passport that allows it access to the worlds of happiness, harmony and spiritual fortune. The connection with the spiritual power of the Supreme enables the mind to maintain its spiritual awareness and experience. God's great, unlimited spiritual strength holds the mind focused, so that it develops and nurtures and releases its formerly dormant powers. The clear, integrated and aligned mind is able to perform actions that end its connection with the past and accumulate the return of a positive nature and a positive future. With this return to a holistic state, the mind moves into contentment and a more meaningful spiritual state of joyful happiness.

With the rapidly disintegrating energy systems of the world and with increasing scenes of confusion and personal loss, the angelic mind becomes a spiritual holding point – a source of hope and support. Stabilized in the unchanging and unlimited world of spiritual light it becomes the medium of God's help and returning love.

As we have seen, it is only in an environment of silence and purity that the mind aligns its world with that of the Supreme. Thus connected and influenced, the angelic consciousness becomes an outlet of God's celestial love and wisdom. And as if in response to the supplications and sorrows of our increasingly chaotic world, the role of the angel is created and manifests almost like a device of God.

Trusted and empowered, the angelic mind becomes the conduit of God's support to the Earth.

Through insight, the angelic mind is used to translate knowledge and awareness to those lost in the confusion of untruth. Through its power it becomes a lighthouse of regeneration for those trapped in prisons of hopelessness and despair. And through love it becomes a healer for hearts broken and overflowing with sorrow.

Within the fallout of the surrounding chaotic world, where there was only the darkness of hopelessness and despair, the angelic mind works through the pathways of the silent worlds to provide vibrations of power and support. This power brings relief and insight, and evokes hope and inspiration, triggering new enthusiasm and fresh momentum. Like a lighthouse, angelic, subtle and focused thoughts stream out into the darkness of strife-torn lands, dispersing and changing the heavy psychic clouds of fear and sorrow.

Being God-centered and love-centered, the thoughts of the angelic mind speak directly and go deeply into the shattered empty hearts, reviving and recalling old and sacred memories of times of distant beauty, and reminding them of the One who loves them, remembers them and is there for them. Souls are beckoned, guided and welcomed into the harbor of love, the healing haven and a sanctuary of solace that offers a new direction and beginning.

The angelic mind's vibrational energy of pure, positive love dramatically impacts upon the languishing and listless energies of the wandering souls lost in the shadow lands of the lower worlds. It becomes a lifebelt and a lifeboat that offers a resuscitating kiss to all drowning souls.

Practical ways to use the Angelic Mind:

- The subtle angelic state creates an atmosphere of positive influence. Remember that whoever comes into your orbit, either at work or at home, will be supported and influenced by that empowering energy.
- Help those with particular problems, fears and issues by surrounding them with pure, positive and powerful fields of spiritual energy. Help them lift the old mindsets and negative thoughts by giving them the strength and insight to enable them to see and then move into a more desired state.
- To emerge the subtle form of the individual that you're helping you must link in light and power with the Supreme. Place the other person in the light-center of God's pure heart and allow that unlimited love energy to empower them and work directly on their soul's pure consciousness.

Let us sit in silence and reflect for a moment, considering the angelic mind and repeating these thoughts:

Meditation

"An angelic mind is free, detached,
aligned with truth;
it moves between the inner and outer worlds.
It is a mind free of the need for acknowledgment,
praise or the garlands of success,
a mind, subtle and light, carefree and content,
a mind not drawn or trapped by form or role,
nor influenced or deceived by the wonders of the technocratic
*   worlds.*
It is a heart full of happiness, enthusiasm and joy.
An angelic mind is a messenger,
a spiritual go-between,
an ambassador of eternal truth and
the outreach arm of God's pure thought.
It is an embodiment of spiritual power,
an icon enshrined in all beliefs.
It is the returning image,
a long-lost dream,
wonderful,
terrifying,
a destroyer of night,
the bringer of light,
a harbinger of change."

8 The God Knowing Mind

When we think of the term 'unlimited' and try to comprehend what it may encompass, even when using analogy or symbolism, we stretch our imagination to magnitudes of cosmic proportion and hit a wall of mental frustration. For when the limited mind tries to grapple with the infinite, it tries to hold onto and define the impossible. That is the difficulty of trying to perceive the extent and capacity of God's mind and consciousness.

In a limited way we could imagine this Mind to be like a huge and vast ocean that touches every aspect and every part of all land masses. We could imagine it as an ocean that is connected, yet completely separate, with no tides, no waves and no motion. It is like a vast body, completely full and still, whose constant state never fluctuates or wavers but remains steadfast and unchanging in both form and being.

Yet with all this vastness and power that is God, it is incredible, even ironic that we, being the land, can forget this spiritual ocean. The physical ocean is crucial to the land's well-being and existence – its life-giving clouds bring refreshment and power. And so too the ocean-form of the Supreme brings the nurturing waters of awareness and spiritual life to the soul.

It is the ego of physical consciousness that denies the Supreme Ocean, as if desiring to claim His role as its own. Instead it ignores Him and creates countless philosophies to prove He's not there. On turning its back to the Supreme Ocean the ego leaves the land to embrace the repercussions of its decision.

Yet in the stillness of God's ocean there is understanding. It is a knowing that precedes unknowing, an awareness that needs no thought or reflection. In this compassion and constancy of love all mistakes can be rectified and all sorrows healed. For the Supreme ocean never leaves the land; the waves constantly lap against it as a reminder of its love, refreshment and support.

But to know the Supreme ocean in its entirety is possibly beyond our present capacities. With the physical ocean we can focus on and understand fragments in order to appreciate and make greater sense of the whole. So, in our limited way, via the perceptions and links of subtle intellect, we can gain deeper and clearer insights into the beauty of the Supreme mind and person-ality.

Trapped by the effects of its past and the web of its expanding fears and ferocious desires, the physical mind is prevented from acknowledging a Divine existence. Even as the spiritual mind moves away from the confusion of the lower worlds, it has to deal with the blocks and delusions of the ego, which can deflect the aspirant consciousness into the aridity of self-importance and God-like fantasies.

Entry into the inner world of the Supreme is through light, humility and emptiness, for the mind first has to be honest and true, free of conceits and desires and with a heart that is pure and clear. When light connects with light, a union of pure minds occurs. It is in this harmony, unity and closeness that a window of insight can be opened into God's divine nature and consciousness.

Once placed in the mind of God, the spiritual mind is drawn into the infinity of God's being. It is an unending mind without boundaries – a vast, seamless silence of unlimited bliss. Here there are no plans or speculations, no philosophy or questions. The mind of God can be seen like a vast cosmic sun of knowing, perfectly positioned, stable and still. It is completely absorbed by a universe of truth and blissful contentment.

On entering this realm of pre-mythic wonder the mind is drawn into a region of deep, eternal silence. The pure and unlimited nature of the Supreme catalyzes and transforms the mind's patterns of perception and thinking. External consciousness is submerged in this vast sea of inner consciousness. The willing mind gives itself to this regenerating energy-flow of infinite love. Such is the impact of this pure energy that the mind is reborn. It falls into a pre-experience state of consciousness and undergoes an energy synthesis, as if being absorbed into the oneness of a universal force. As the mind is harmonized and brought into equilibrium it starts to awaken to its future experience.

For the mind, the realization is dramatic and profound. Having previously searched and reached out for meaning and experience, it aspires to the concept of transcendence and is suddenly within the sacred presence of Supreme Consciousness. It links to the Supreme mind, a position once thought of as impossible. Through this union the mind moves into knowing and awareness and its consciousness extends to fullness. What was unknown now becomes known. Acceptance and appreciation emerge as the natural order of the spiritual world is observed. And in that awareness time's great cycle is grasped and realized, and past, present and future are seen through the clarity of the divine intellect. Thus, eternity is embraced and the mind moves into freedom. In this synchronicity the mind experiences an incredible empowerment and transformation. In touching the heart-center of the Supreme the mind opens its consciousness to the universal world of truth and spiritual power.

However, insights into the direct mind and inner world of God can only be speculative because two huge experiences take place simultaneously. Firstly, when we embrace the elevated company of the Supreme, indescribable feelings and awareness rush in. Secondly comes a tremendous release of the soul's own pure consciousness and the activation of its inner wisdom and higher nature. It is through this emergence of the mind's own divine nature, which filters everything through its own experience and perceptions, that we clearly discern how God's mind functions and how His attitude frames world consciousness.

Whatever our individual limitations and restrictions, it is only from the manifestation of the angelic consciousness that the mind gains a vision and some understanding of the workings and power of God's great mind. In the impact of this sacred union the Supreme identity transfers. The mind, egoless and empty, is receptive to that divine imprint. Its mindset becomes an identikit of God's pure mind and consciousness.

From the citadel of God's pure heart, in this unity of awareness, the mind that understands the mind of God experiences the indescribable power and beauty of God's benevolent being. There is the realization and awareness of the unending, eternal nature of being, the unchanging nature of the cosmic soul and the great movement of the recurring play that spins in a never-ending cycle.

And from the high vantage point of this loving and detached awareness, the mind observes others below clamoring with their calls for wealth and status and filled with the frantic fears of mere mortality. Yet in the company of the Great Truth, and as if seeing through God's eyes, the mind recognizes their futility and insignificance. It sees how all plans and issues emerge, then merge together before finally disappearing like driftwood into the great river of eternity.

For knowing there is no death, no loss, no gain, no better or worse and realizing that it is just a play of coming and going, a play of losing and finding, a play of happiness and sorrow, so in the company of God, the mind smiles and knows that everything is fine and everything is well, for all has been and will be and still is, just a game.

Practical ways to use the mind that understands the mind of God:

- Think on God and about God and your world changes; you have moved into the vastness of the unlimited.
- Experiencing God's connection and company, can there be any difficulties or obstacles to block your path?
- Through your awareness you bring God back into the world of others.

Let us sit in silence and meditate for a moment, on our connection with God, by repeating these thoughts:

Meditation

> *"Here in this sacred union,*
> *I begin to glimpse the vastness of eternity*
> *and the immensity of God's great mind*
> *and spiritual power.*

Then all my fears,
all my worries and anxieties
all my desires for this and that
and all the issues I get caught up with
quickly diminish
and fall away.
And I become free,
free to experience
the wonders of the spiritual world."

9 The Future Mind

All things are subject to change. And as all things change, the mind balances precariously between many fast-shifting scenes and life's trapeze becomes tricky. The mind may be knocked here and there by the influences of its world just like a shuttlecock, and it experiences the repercussions of this vulnerability through a huge number of disabling effects.

As the mind journeys into silence, relinquishing its attachment and associations with physical form, it is able to reach deeper into the unlimited through its union with God's power, thus bringing an end to all inner disturbance and fluctuation, to arrive finally at the realm of metaphysical stillness. In this stillness the machinery of the mind changes orientation and the whirring machinations of planning and projection slow and finally stop. To many, this may appear to be the termination of physical life, as if it were given the last vestigial rites before the moment of death. And in many respects it is a death – the death of the old mind, and its mindset and attitudes. It is the demise of negative consciousness and all its painful associations and a rebirth into a new family of values, awareness and truth.

In this state the future mind is free, satisfied and centered within a holding force field of non-material, pure spiritual energy that maintains and reinforces this consciousness of pure being. It is this experience, this realized awareness, that is the seed of nature and enables the returning mind to create a life based on the principles of spiritual understanding, abundance and inner contentment.

With consciousness so firmly rooted, there are no desires, no regrets, no disappointments, no negative history and no sorrow, for sorrow is resolutely encamped in the citadels of the past. The divinized intellect has the strength and awareness not to yield to the pull of memory. Each scene and interaction becomes like a stepping stone to the next stage and there is no going back. Unlike Lot's wife, there is no looking back to block and trap the soul. At this stage of its journey, the mind has no reflective thoughts about what occurs because each new scenario fully envelops and holds it in its uniqueness and beauty. With the future mind totally centered and absorbed in its present, time loses its tyranny and like the world of nature becomes completely aligned and focused, intrinsically woven into the delight and joy of each moment.

Alert and highly tuned in this pivot of balanced focus, the intellect assimilates the scene, circumstances and personalities and from its accumulated wisdom-store responds intuitively and spontaneously, able to give its whole attention and energy to support, appreciate and enjoy. Such is the acceptance of what is being revealed and what is being experienced that there is no criticism, no desire to change and no ego to interfere. Thoughts are expressed through delight and happiness, and actions performed in alignment and support. Thus energy, health and relationships are never compromised.

In the past when the intellect was fractured, submerged and marginalized to the outer perimeters of awareness and control, the mind was isolated and vulnerable, invaded and overrun. Yet the future mind regains the kingdom. Like a restored ruler, the intellect returns from its banishment and just as Odysseus shoots the suitors for his kingdom with the arrows of wisdom, it is seated once again on its throne of self-awareness.

With balance and control firmly held, the mind no longer topples into free-fall flights of worry caused by unnecessary and unwanted fears and wild suppositions. The turbulent seas of old nature and reactive responses become stilled and are no longer accessed. Inner knowing and inner wisdom, filled within the deep portals of the revived intellect, allow no leeway, no speculative storms can spring up and create havoc on the now tranquil shores of experience.

In the inner kingdom of future mind everything moves into place, everything is in agreement. Everything automatically responds to the restoration of order. There are no disputes or vying for precedence or domination. It is a jigsaw with all the pieces in place; there are no margins, no options. There is no need to plan, to judge, to reconstruct. In fact there is not much need to even think at all. All is well, for the mind is happy and content. It is a fragrant flower in the flower garden of beauty, harmony and perfect order.

Practical ways to use the Future Mind:

- Wherever you may find yourself, remember that you can be free from that environment. Rather than experience yourself as a set of reactive appendages and effects, separate your consciousness and just be who you are.
- Hold the thought of love and hold the experience of love and move into that feeling and awareness, gradually expanding and extending the orb ofits influence. Within love you are centered and surrounded, and you are that experience.
- There is no need for thought or associations of comparison. Just hold and stay within the field of being, observing and interacting with love.

Let us sit in silence and reflect for a moment, considering the future mind and repeating these thoughts:

Meditation

The stillness of all things
pulls me into silence.
I glide into that space
and become part of the stillness,
where everything is held as
part of a perfect
mosaic of natural order.
I hold that moment.
I feel part of everything
and everything feels a part of me.
I expand into all
and I reduce the all
into the essence of my being.
And all things are as they are.

Epilogue

"A lighthouse of love, the crystal mind stretches, searches, spreads its rays of hope and guidance out into the dark troubled seas of the world, where the storm-tossed, storm-lost souls try frantically to reach the long-sought haven of the peaceful mind.

And these travellers of the unlimited seas now crippled and disabled by the ravages of the journey and the depredations of influence, call out, searching for help, for answers, for solutions to their predicaments.

Through the subtle pathways of the angelic world, the spiritual mind reaches and finds and leads the souls' stricken vessels to the repair yards of inner light, to heal the hearts long broken and to fix the faith long lost.

Through its clarity and self-awareness, the spiritual mind becomes a mirror for those who cannot see the way, who are unclear and confused; it resolves the causes of accumulated sorrow and eases those who feel trapped by its weight.

And in all this, the spiritual mind neither sees nor holds, for it is solely focused and absorbed in the joy and beauty of God's great light. And yet, it is remembered, revered and recalled by others. For when the stars of the evening sky glitter and sparkle in the highest heavens, they invoke and call out, triggering memories of their once great acts."

About Raja Yoga

Raja Yoga is an ancient system of bringing the mind and emotions into balance in order to develop knowledge and wisdom and gain a deep understanding of the self. Through the simple practice of silent meditation and by turning your consciousness inward you can bring the mind and emotions into balance and become the creator of your own thoughts and feelings.

About Brahma Kumaris:

The Brahma Kumaris World Spiritual University is an international organization working at all levels of society for positive change. Established in 1937, the University now has more than 8,500 centers in over 100 countries.

Acknowledging the intrinsic worth and goodness of the inner self, the University teaches a practical method of meditation that helps people to cultivate their inner strengths and values.

The University has local centers around the world offering courses and seminars that encourage spirituality in daily life and cover topics such as positive thinking, anger management, stress relief and self-esteem, among others. This spiritual approach is also brought into healthcare, social work, education, prisons and other community settings.

The University's Academy in Mount Abu, Rajasthan, India, offers individuals from all backgrounds a variety of life-long learning opportunities to help them recognize their inherent qualities and abilities in order to make the most of their lives. The University also supports the Global Hospital and Research Centre in Mount Abu.

All courses and activities are offered free of charge.

www.bkwsu.org

www.bkwsu.org/uk

How to Find Out More

World Headquarters

PO Box No 2, Mount Abu 307501, RAJASTHAN, INDIA
Tel: (+91) 2974 - 238261 to 68 Fax: (+91) 2974 - 238883
E-mail: abu@bkivv.org

International Co-ordinating Office
& Regional Office For Europe And The Middle East

Global Co-operation House, 65-69 Pound Lane, London, NW10
2HH, UK
Tel: (+44) 20 8727 3350 Fax: (+44) 20 8727 3351
E-mail: london@bkwsu.org

Africa

Global Museum for a Better World, Maua Close, off Parklands
Road, Westlands
PO Box 123, Sarit Centre, Nairobi, Kenya
Tel: (+254) 20 - 374 3572 Fax: (+254) 20 - 374 3885
E-mail: nairobi@bkwsu.org

Australia and South East Asia

78 Alt Street, Ashfield, Sydney, NSW 2131, Australia
Tel: (+61) 2 9716 7066 Fax: (+61) 2 9716 7795
E-mail: ashfield@au.bkwsu.org

The Americas and The Caribbean

Global Harmony House, 46 S. Middle Neck Road, Great Neck,
NY 11021, USA
Tel: (+1) 516 773 0971 Fax: (+1) 516 773 0976
E-mail: newyork@bkwsu.org

Russia, CIS and the Baltic Countries

2 Gospitalnaya Ploschad, Build 1, Moscow - 111020, Russia

Tel: (+7) 499 263 02 47 Fax: (+7) 499 261 32 24

E-mail: moscow@bkwsu.org

Website: www.bkpublications.com
E-mail: enquiries@bkpublications.com